THE
STENCIL BOOK

THE STENCIL BOOK

With over 30 stencils to cut out or trace

Amelia Saint George

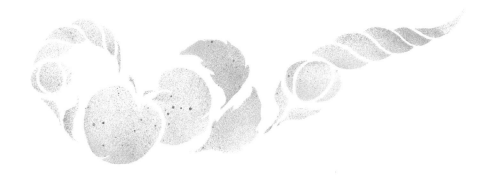

Photographs by Jan Baldwin

SHELTON BOOKS

To Mummy, Thomas, Abigail and Tithaine

Text by Penny David
Art editor Heather Garioch
Editor Emma Callery
Production Shane Lask
Stencil artwork Roy Flooks
Editorial assistant Simon Willis

First published in 1988 by
Conran Octopus Limited
37 Shelton Street
London WC2H 9HN

This paperback edition published
in 1990 by Conran Octopus Limited.
Reprinted 1990, 1991 (twice), 1992 (twice), 1993 (twice),
1994 (four times), 1995, 1996 (three times), 1997, 1998
Text © Conran Octopus Limited 1988

ISBN 1-85029-959-5

Typeset by Bookworm
Printed in China

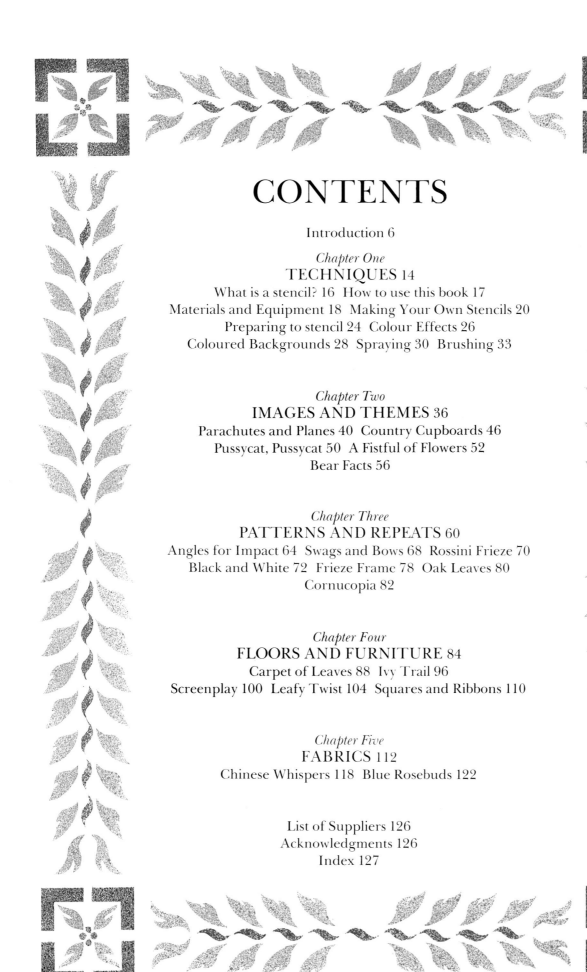

CONTENTS

INTRODUCTION

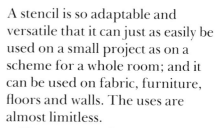

Stencilling is rewarding straight away. You can begin with a simple stencil such as this strawberry plant (SEE STENCILS ON PAGES 106 AND 107) *and immediately make something that is not only attractive but unique: for instance, it is easy to personalize bland, mass-produced objects* (opposite).

Stencilling is a very special aspect of interior decorating. With stencils you make your own truly unique mark on your surroundings because *you* choose your motif, *you* decide where it goes and *you* do the colouring. Whether you decide upon one of my stencils in this book, whether you copy a motif from somewhere else, or whether you use an original stencil you have designed yourself, the way you apply it always makes it your own.

A stencil is so adaptable and versatile that it can just as easily be used on a small project as on a scheme for a whole room; and it can be used on fabric, furniture, floors and walls. The uses are almost limitless.

To me, a stencil is simply a design form which can be altered and used in the way which is most suitable for the circumstances it is being used in. Working as an interior designer, I so often hear, 'Oh! I like the pattern, but the colours are not right', or, 'The colours are good, but the overall pattern is too busy for my room.' However, since a stencil is so versatile, these problems are easily overcome and you will always have the opportunity of planning the exact effect required. After reading through this book you will soon find that should you wish to visually alter the proportions of a wall by adding a dado rail or vertical lines, or unify your room by stencilling on to curtains, cushions and upholstery then these effects are all within your grasp.

Stencils can be made to 'move' in the way you want them to. For instance, a teddy bear can be made to sit, stand and walk simply by manipulating the same stencil – indeed, all my stencils are designed with just this flexibility in mind. With careful masking, anything from a single leaf to a glorious bouquet can be applied using only one, simple idea. The subtle use of colour will also alter the 'look' of the end result and it is well worth practising with all the different kinds of paint available. Whether you choose to use spray paint,

Children love stencils, particularly ones that reflect their favourite stories and characters. Generous-sized stencils are not only decorative, but often improve proportions, visually anchoring child-sized furniture in adult-sized rooms.

fabric paint or stencil crayons, take a detailed look at each – there are advantages to them all.

Today's stencilling is highly sophisticated, going well in chic town houses and international apartments as well as in country cottages. It is a top designer trademark as well as a project for the do-it-yourself home decorator.

Stencilled images can be exciting (even erotic) rather than tame and mundane. Their colouring can be subtle, misty and ethereal rather than crude. Their outlines can be hazy and indistinct, or crisp and sharp – challenging with metallic textures and arresting contrasts. Instead of monotonous static motifs, stencils can be so skilfully used that it is a puzzle to see where the repeats begin and end.

When someone new asks me to do some stencilling for them, one of my first tasks is to 'read' their home to see what their ideas about style might be. Everyone's aim is comfort, and everyone sets about achieving it in a way that best approximates to their ideal way of life. People's homes provide me with clues, not only in the styles of furniture and objects, but also in the colours and textures with which they surround themselves. I have evolved a sort of shorthand to classify four general styles to help me know how to set about designing a motif and then interpret it in terms of colours, textures, formality of arrangement and so on. Remember – these styles are as much about what people like and aspire to as what they have actually got around them.

What I call 'farm house' involves natural materials and colours – brick, slate and wood floors; rush matting; whitewash and wooden beams. Most of the essential elements are traditional. There are nooks and crannies, winding staircases, all lending themselves to stencilling – particularly with simple images depicting plants, flowers, herbs and natural objects.

My 'country house' category has a more spacious feeling of history – a mellow atmosphere of the faded gentility of the manor house or old rectory, with special pieces of furniture and family portraits. Floral print fabrics and flowers from the garden – perhaps gently stylized, and harmonizing with architecture and furniture – often suggest stencilling themes.

'Town house' is smarter, more hard-edged: a sophisticated mixture of modern and antique that marries original features such as cornices and fireplaces with up-to-the-minute gadgets and luxury fittings. Stencilling offers ingenious and sometimes witty ways of effecting transitions and blending old and new.

'International' is my shorthand for contemporary living, in a home that could be anywhere. We troop from place to place gathering inspiration here, mementoes there, and incorporate them within

Pattern can be built up in a casual or systematic way by repeating individual stencil motifs. Plants and flowers make almost universally popular themes, and designs based on them can be as stylized or as naturalistic as you please.

whatever four walls we find around us. Stencilling is about creating an illusion of unity in this disparate world.

Most homes reflect a mixture of compromises on these styles, depending on different personalities, requirements and circumstances. Despite this, I find the basic tactic to work well and perhaps it is something you could adopt in order to settle on a stencilling style that suits you.

Loose garlands of lilies in an informal frieze bring a country-house feel to a city bedroom. By reversing the stencils and varying angles, the repeats are difficult to discern.

One of the few basic rules for successful stencilling is that the design should work in its context, so that stencilling on walls, say, becomes part of the shell of a room, taking on an architectural quality and becoming more than just a superficial decoration. As with all the best-designed things, a stencilled device should seem

almost inevitable – since you are calling the tune, you can choose something appropriate, and adapt it to suit. The satisfaction in the result is equivalent to the difference between off-the-peg average fit and perfect bespoke tailoring – maybe even, if you cut your own stencils from scratch, designer originals.

Make stencilling work for you. Take repeating designs, for instance. If you had wanted remorseless all-over patterning, with precise mechanical accuracy, you might as well have used printed wallpaper, scissors and paste. When you build pattern with a stencil, however, you conjure with space and the motif itself to make the effect seem right, so that your design belongs to the surface it embellishes, and yet has a life, a degree of movement and vitality. This applies whether you are stencilling an ebullient swag or a restrained classic border design; whether your pattern is free-flowing and open, or more formal and closed. The tactics for adjusting pattern to fit the space that are described in Chapter Three prevent those dreadful stencillers' *faux pas* with motifs cut off in their prime.

The effect of choosing some intrinsically relevant decorative element for a stencil (taking your cue from fabric, furnishings or architecture) and making it echo around the room will always add up to more than the sum of the parts. For example, a garland of leaves to soften the hard lines of a frame around a picture could either come from the picture itself, or from elsewhere in the room, so marrying the picture to the room. A device stencilled on walls or furniture could be adapted to provide both a repeated border and a little

Above: *The colouring modulates gently as the stencil reaches different areas of the room. The frieze loops down dramatically above the bed-head, the room's focal point.*

Left: *Details such as stems and stamens are added with a second stencil.*

Gradually you learn to design stencils to suit particular situations, adapting them to fit into awkward shapes such as this chest of drawers.

all-over motif for some fabric – curtains, tablecloth or duvet cover – in the same room. Such coherence is the hallmark of good design.

Another classic feature of good design is understatement –

New materials like car spray paints and acetate film put the process within anybody's reach, and potentially put the results into the professional league. You can make a stencilling project your life's work, or you can do it in minutes and cover it all up with a new coat of paint next week. You can have the idea in the morning and be looking at the finished result that evening, although actually I'd advise you to wait at least overnight – pin up a photocopy or a practice-run of your design painted on lining paper and let the impression take you unawares. Either you will know it is right, or you will get a better idea of how to modify it.

Patterned backgrounds (opposite) *can be tailored to the precise sizes and proportions you want.*

knowing when to stop, keeping it simple. Stencilling is so easy, but the benefit of a mature design vision enables you to compose with stencils and enhance your surroundings to the fullest effect – without overdoing it.

I have tried to include plenty of tips in the following chapters – things I have learnt from experience. However much theory you absorb, you will inevitably be putting it into practice in your home, in your own particular way. I can only guide you on that way. That is why the projects later in this book are loosely framed – really I don't need to tell you exactly what colour or size your finished stencil needs to be.

The first chapter, like a basic stencilling lesson, tells you all the techniques you need to know. After that you are *in situ*, with stencilling projects for you to follow yourself or to call on for inspiration. Chapters Two and Three look at stencils used either singly and/or as repeats. Chapters Four and Five consider some special cases – stencilling on materials such as wood and fabric.

Stencilling is fun and can be used from floor to ceiling, from the sitting room to the playroom. A clean method of adding charm and individuality to your home, it is quick and easy. Go and try.

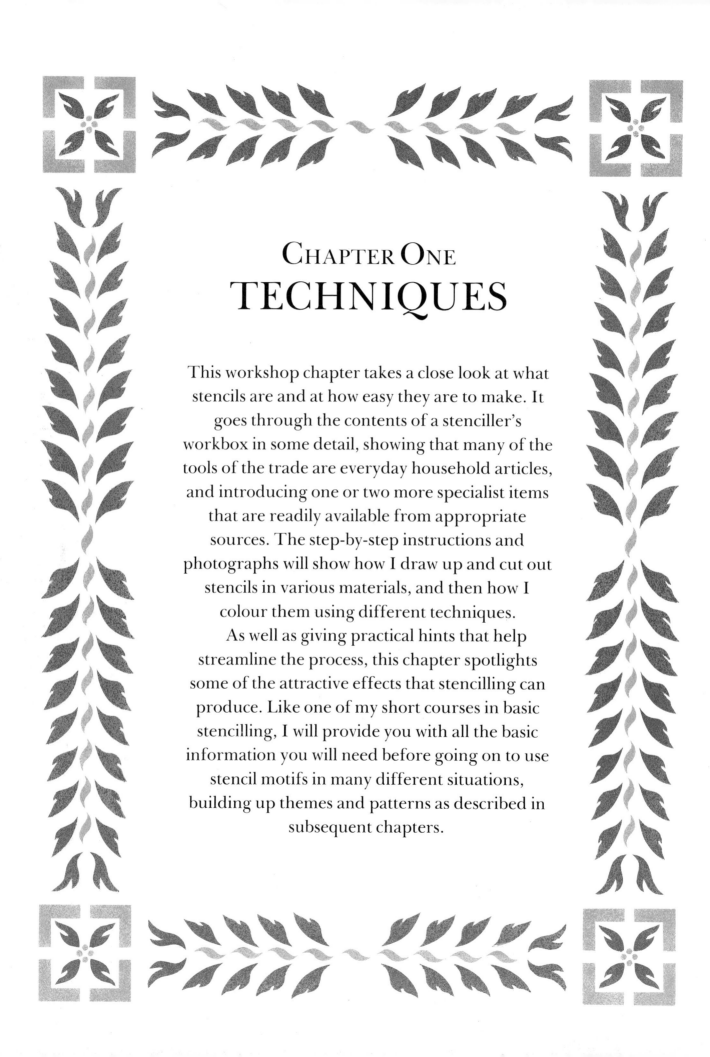

CHAPTER ONE
TECHNIQUES

This workshop chapter takes a close look at what stencils are and at how easy they are to make. It goes through the contents of a stenciller's workbox in some detail, showing that many of the tools of the trade are everyday household articles, and introducing one or two more specialist items that are readily available from appropriate sources. The step-by-step instructions and photographs will show how I draw up and cut out stencils in various materials, and then how I colour them using different techniques.

As well as giving practical hints that help streamline the process, this chapter spotlights some of the attractive effects that stencilling can produce. Like one of my short courses in basic stencilling, I will provide you with all the basic information you will need before going on to use stencil motifs in many different situations, building up themes and patterns as described in subsequent chapters.

WHAT IS A STENCIL?

Think of a stencil as simply a pattern of holes cut into a sheet of resilient waterproof material which acts as a supporting frame. Colour is brushed or sprayed through the holes, recreating the pattern on the surface beneath. As the stencil is cut from a substantial material, it can be repositioned and used again and again, either identically or with variations. Traditional stencilling often uses a succession of different sheets for different colours, building up superimposed designs. Attractive results can, however, be more easily achieved with a single stencil sheet and an imaginative use of colour – as most of the stencils in this book demonstrate.

Stencil designs

All stencil motifs consist of a series of 'windows' through which you apply paint to a surface, and a system of 'bridges' separating the windows. The bridges are both structural (strengthening the cut-away areas of the stencil) and aesthetic (defining different parts of the motif, and often separating different-coloured panels). In well-designed stencils, the bridges seem an intrinsic part of the whole, contributing a fluid, rhythmic quality to the motif. They often occur where one shape passes behind another, creating depth of field. In plant forms such as leaves, veining provides a ready-made network of natural lines that can be followed for bridges. Alternatively, abstract geometrical motifs use the bridges purely as pattern.

In their basic form, stencil outlines are simply contrasts between solid area and window, but when subtly coloured they become fully fledged designs, potentially rich in movement and three-dimensional qualities.

The free flowing shapes of plant forms – such as this trailing ivy (featured on pages 96 and 99) – provide many natural breaks for bridges.

16

HOW TO USE THIS BOOK

Two sorts of stencil are included in this book – you can choose between experimenting with the simple do-it-yourself method and taking advantage of the even simpler, ready-made options printed on tracing paper on pages 42–3, 74–5, 90–1 and 106–7.

Making your own stencils

Many of the designs shown in the projects are clearly printed on the page alongside the photographs, for you to trace. If the image is already the size you want, you can just transfer this outline to your chosen stencilling material (see pages 21–3) and cut it out.

You may want to enlarge or reduce the image as described on page 20 before transferring it to stencilling material. You may even want to adapt the design slightly, cut further repeats of a pattern, or make other adjustments of your own: all these alterations can be made at the tracing stage, before cutting the actual stencil.

The method for making this category of stencils is the same one that you would use if you wanted to copy a motif from another source, or to adapt a design you had drawn yourself.

Preparing the 'ready-to-use' stencils

These are specially designed for you to remove from the book and cut out to use as actual same-size stencils right away. The special heavy-duty tracing paper on which they are printed is substantial enough to withstand about a dozen repeats: if you anticipate doing a good many more, it might be as well

to transfer the design to stronger material as described on pages 21–3.

Completing the stencils

Whichever way you make your stencils, colour them according to one of the techniques described on pages 30–5. When I work, I tend to concentrate on the tried and tested techniques I have found work for me. Colouring, for example. Occasionally I use crayons or acrylic paints, but as a professional who needs to work at speed, I generally prefer cans of spray paint. I advise you to read through the information on applying colour, then experiment and see which medium you enjoy most. In the same way, try out different kinds of stencilling materials and different types of cutting tools.

The Frieze Frame stencil on page 42 is a multiple stencil, designed to be coloured in two separate layers. One tinted outline shows the windows for one stencil in the usual way; another indicates windows for the second stencil. You will need to trace one set of outlines as described on pages 21–3. The other outline provided is, of course, ready to cut out and use straight away.

This stencil is also a section of a repeat, and a dotted line shows the positioning of the next repeat.

MATERIALS AND EQUIPMENT

Stencil boards

All sorts of materials have been used for stencils, from fine sheet metal to varnished cartridge paper. The ready-to-use stencils in this book are printed on heavy-duty opaque tracing paper of the sort that is available from graphics suppliers. This is durable enough for up to a dozen or so repeats.

For making your own stencils from the traceable outlines in this book – or, indeed, from your own designs – choose between two classic materials sold specifically for the purpose by art suppliers and good stationers – oiled manila board and transparent acetate.

Oiled board (manila card, waterproofed with linseed oil) is relatively cheap, durable and tough, but not difficult to cut. The thicker gauge is more often on sale, but the finer gauge is adequate for most stencils, and is easier to cut and fold.

Acetate is more expensive and relatively difficult to cut well into intricate shapes. It also tends to rip easily.   Choose the thicker gauge for a large design that is to be handled a good deal, but remember that it is difficult to bend into awkward corners. The thinner gauge is useful for smaller, less frequent repeats. An advantage of

using acetate is that when positioning the stencil for colouring you can see the previous stencil on the wall – until layers of paint make it virtually opaque.

A variation on conventional acetate is single-matt, translucent design film, available from graphics suppliers. This is matt on one side and glossy on the other. The matt side is easier to use when cutting, since the knife does not slip so much. Another advantage is that you can also use a pencil on the matt side.

Stencilling brushes

In order to stipple paint vertically into stencil windows without letting it seep under the edges, you need specially designed brushes – round or tube-shaped, with stiff bristles cut straight across at the end. The best (but most expensive) brushes are made of natural gray or black hog hairs; those with synthetic bristles are considerably cheaper – but are less long-lasting. Brushes come in a wide range of sizes, and you should choose ones appropriate to the scale of your design. You will find that you will generally need a couple of brushes when working – one for the light colours, and one for the dark.

Clean your brushes carefully after use, using soapy water (or the solvent recommended on the paint label) to remove every trace of colour. Leave them to dry with an elastic band round the bristles to keep them straight, and make sure that they are perfectly dry before using again. Do make sure that the elastic band isn't too tight as this will spoil your brushes.

You can wrap cling film closely round the bristles to prevent the paint from drying during any short interruptions to your stencilling.

BASIC EQUIPMENT

This is purely a list of the basic equipment needed when stencilling. On the following pages I describe their uses in greater detail.

For copying or resizing a design

drawing paper	erasers
tracing paper	felt-tip pens
pencils,	masking tape

For transferring a design to stencil board

traced design

oiled stencil board at least 5 cm/2 in larger each way than design	soft pencil masking tape

For transferring a design to acetate

original design

acetate sheet at least 5 cm/2 in larger each way than design	felt-tip or technical drawing pen

For cutting out a stencil

craft knife or paper scalpel, plus new blades masking tape or clear tape for repairing mistakes	PVC 'self-healing' cutting mat or glass sheet with edges protected

For positioning a stencil

tape measure, ruler or straight edge chalk or soft pencil for marking	spirit level plumb line string

For sticking a stencil in position

repositionable spray adhesive

For colouring a stencil

aerosol spray paints

newsapapers and masking tape lining paper for testing spray effects	cellulose thinners/nail varnish remover, to remove paint if necessary

OR

stencil crayons

several stencil brushes	white spirit, to clean brushes

OR

acrylic paints

several stencil brushes palettes, lollipop sticks,	storage jars etc. for mixing paper towels

OR

fabric paints

several stencil brushes

For protecting a stencil

clear polyurethane varnish	paint or varnish brush

MAKING YOUR OWN STENCILS

Resizing a design

The traditional – and rather laborious – way of enlarging a design is to draw a regular grid over the original and to copy the design, square by square, on to a larger grid. Once the copying is complete, draw over the lines of the enlarged design to make sure they are fluid and continuous. Obviously, you can reverse the process to reduce the size of a design and the method also allows you to change proportion by drawing from a square grid to a rectangular one, and of course,

vice versa too.

A second way of sizing up a design and keeping its proportions is to use the enlarging facility of a photocopying machine, setting it to the percentage enlargement you want. You may have to do this in several stages or in several sections, jigsaw-style.

Either way, look at your resized drawing with a critical eye to make sure that it works in design terms. If the change of scale is dramatic, you may need to adjust the width of bridges – or create new ones – to suit the new design.

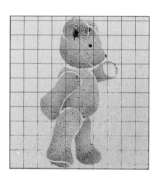

This smiling teddy bear – to be found on pages 56–9 – has been simply enlarged using the grid method described above.

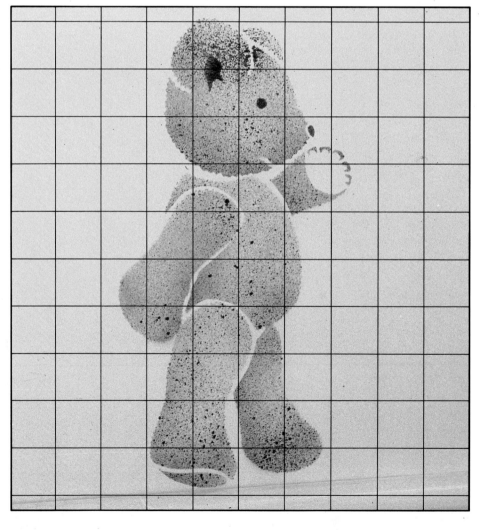

Tracing the design

This basic step is necessary whether you are copying an image from this book or from another source to use as the same size, or as a prelude to altering the size. Tracing is straightforward enough but it is well worth using masking tape to hold the tracing paper in place over the original. The lines on the tracing will serve as cutting lines for the stencil, so make them smooth.

(Keep your tracing. Should you need to make a duplicate stencil, this will be a more reliable source than copying off a previously cut stencil. Tracings are also invaluable for storage: sandwich them between used stencils to prevent them sticking together.)

Transferring the design to acetate

The advantage of using acetate is that you can trace your design directly on to it. Lay the sheet of acetate over the design, anchor it down with masking tape and use a felt-tip or technical drawing pen which is suitable for acetate to trace the design. Shade in the areas to be cut out to help you see more clearly which areas are to be removed.

Transferring the design to stencil board

On the reverse side of the tracing, go over the lines of the design with a soft-leaded pencil. Lay the tracing right way up on the stencil board and secure with masking tape. Draw over the lines once more with an ordinary pencil: a faint outline will be transferred to the stencil board. Remove the tracing and firm up the lines. It is very helpful to shade in the areas to be cut out as windows – particularly for fine designs.

Cutting out stencils

The cutting tools for any material – whether it be stencil board, acetate or the tracing paper of the ready-to-use stencils in this book – are the same: either a lightweight craft knife or a paper scalpel, whichever you find the most comfortable. Whichever you choose must be sharp: so always keep a supply of renewable blades handy.

Suitable cutting surfaces are vital with such sharp tools, both to protect your working surface and to preserve the blade's sharpness as much as possible. Special-purpose PVC 'self-healing' cutting mats (available from graphics or artists' suppliers, or good stationers' shops) are expensive, but they are durable, not slippery, and they don't blunt the blade.

Alternatively, cut on a sheet of thick glass with the edges ground or protected with tape: tinted glass is safer, since it is more easily seen. (There is an additional advantage when cutting an acetate stencil on glass: you can lay the acetate and glass directly over your drawn-out design, and omit the stage of transferring your design on to the acetate.)

Practise your cutting action. Take it slowly and get used to the amount of even pressure you need to exert.

Repairs and joins

If you make a mistake while cutting, or tear a bridge while handling a stencil, stick tape firmly over the break on both sides, and recut the adjacent windows. Use masking tape for stencil board, and clear tape for either acetate or tracing paper.

It is also possible to join sheets with the appropriate tape if you need to cut a stencil larger than you have materials for.

TRACING ON TO STENCIL BOARD

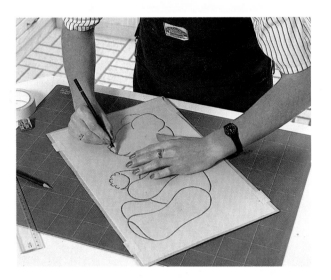

1 Cut a piece of stencil board to a size slightly larger than your design. Attach the tracing to it, after going over the lines of the design on the back with a soft-leaded pencil.

CUTTING OUT STENCILS

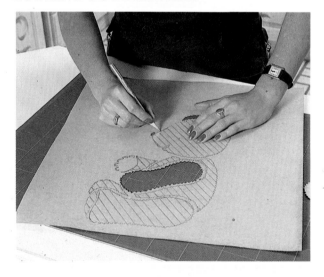

1 Steady the stencil with your spare hand and start at the top or far edge of a shaded-in shape (e.g. the point of a leaf). Draw the blade in the direction of your cutting arm – and always away from the steadying fingers of your spare hand – in a fluent, relaxed movement. You have more control when you use the cutting tool in this direction, so always turn the stencil rather than the knife when you need to change direction.

2 Using the same soft-leaded pencil, draw over the design once more – this time on the right side. You will find that the line on the underside is transferred to the stencil board.

3 If the outline isn't very clear, quickly go over the marks directly on to the stencil board to firm them up. If you don't do this before cutting, you might inadvertantly find yourself smudging a design later on, so losing some fine detail.

2 Try to complete each curve in a single stroke, without taking the blade in and out of the stencil: whenever you do this in mid-line, minute nicks in the window edge will mean that paint will seep under the edge, so smudging the smooth outline.

3 Cut the smaller elements of an intricate design before the larger shapes so that the stencil retains its strength as long as possible during the cutting process. For the same reason, begin at the centre and work outwards. Be sure to leave a substantial margin around the cut-out shapes, again for strength.

PREPARING TO STENCIL

Planning and positioning
Establish some guidelines for overall positioning before you start painting, using a soft pencil or light chalk. Good planning means that if you stencil a motif the wrong way up or back to front, it is because you intended to do so. Ultimately, the distribution of your stencilling depends on your overall design, but here are some general principles:

Centring Finding the centre of a square or rectangle is best done by marking where two diagonals cross. On a large surface like a wall or floor, the easiest way to do this is to pin two pieces of string across the diagonals; or; of course, there is always the good old-fashioned tape measure. Remember, though, that the *true* centre may not be the visual focal point if other aspects are asymmetrical – e.g. if there is a doorway to one side.

Verticals Hang a plumb line from the top of the wall and ask a helper to hold the line at the bottom. Mark the wall at intervals with a pencil or piece of chalk.

Horizontals Using a yardstick, or anything else with a straight edge, and a spirit level mark lines on the wall in a similar way.

Regular spacing in a border
Calculate the number of times a complete motif will fit into the space. Working from the centre outwards, mark the position for the central motif, and then mark positions on either side of this, increasing or decreasing the space between repeats to fill the space evenly. Consider inserting additional motifs at the ends, or between motifs, if the planned positioning seems to be too gappy.

All-over designs Decide on spacing in the same way, then mark a grid of accurate horizontal and vertical guidelines. To do this, begin with vertical lines at either side and then measure the necessary distances up from the floor. After drawing one horizontal line, using a yardstick, check with a T-square that it is at right angles to the verticals. Add further horizontals and verticals at the required intervals.

With careful planning, it is possible to ensure neat corners and evenly spaced designs, as illustrated with this Leafy Twist (see pages 74, 104 and 109).

Remember . . .

● that in many buildings – particularly old ones – walls are not necessarily vertical (this will be most evident at corners) and nor are ceilings and floors horizontal. A geometrically precise border may need to be a compromise between true right-angles and what is visually acceptable. Free-flowing and asymmetrical designs rather than formal patterns help disguise such problems.

● when stencilling a pattern repeat, measure its position each time from some established constant – the ceiling, the edge of the surface, the horizontal line you marked, rather than from the last motif you did; otherwise you risk compounding any error.

Preparing surfaces

Paintwork must above all be sound, both so that your paint goes on smoothly and so that you do not remove any of it when you pull your stencil off for repositioning. Some people say that you cannot stencil on to glossy paint, but I have found it works perfectly.

Don't stencil on to plastic, vinyl and other synthetic substances and use special ceramic paints if you want to stencil on tiles. However, you may well find that this is not hard-wearing, and so is impractical for most places where you need tiles. For unpainted wooden surfaces, see Chapter Four, and for fabric, see Chapter Five.

Sticking a stencil in position

Many people seem to think masking tape is sufficient to hold a stencil in place while you colour it, but I find there is nothing to beat spray adhesive sold by graphics or artists' suppliers: make sure you buy the kind that allows

repositioning. It forms a close contact with any surface so preventing paint from seeping under the edges of the stencil windows while you work. When you have finished, lift the stencil directly off the surface to avoid smudging and reposition it immediately. With modern paints, sparingly used, there is no delay while you wait for them to dry.

Protect the area around your stencil with newspaper and spray a light, even coat over the stencil from a distance of about 20cm/8in. Should you need to clean off any sprayed adhesive, use white spirit or the solvent recommended by the manufacturer. Always read the safety instructions on the can thoroughly for this product should be used with care.

No alternative to repositionable spray adhesive seems to offer such reliable results – the edges come out clean and crisp, and it is easy to reposition the stencil for the next repeat.

COLOUR EFFECTS

The traditional stencils of folk-art often depended on contrasting areas of densely painted primary hues and were naïve and crude in their effect. They were (and are) charming in their place – which is not the sophisticated interiors of today's homes. The paints now available allow a degree of control that means that stencilling can be as subtle and tasteful in colour terms as any other designer-conscious aspect of interior decoration – from contemporary distressed paint finishes on walls to harmoniously coordinated printed fabrics.

'Movement' is what characterizes the best stencilled designs. Obviously this is partly a matter of line, but it is more often a result of skilful use of colour, either as tonal contrast (lighter and darker shades of a single colour) – or the harmonious use of multicolours.

While the following pages explain in detail the different options for applying colour, it is hard to stress strongly enough how important it is not to use too much paint: the effects discussed here depend on a light and subtle touch with the stencil brush or spray can.

Tonal contrast

Even an intrinsically static motif like a monochrome fleur-de-lis can be made to seem three-dimensional and lively by careful application of paint. An even coverage will flatten a shape, so deploy tonal contrast to imitate light and shade, creating an impression of relief. In a stencil window depicting a rounded shape, concentrate the deeper tone and heavier paint coverage on the side away from the source of light or towards the base. It is important to keep highlights light, with the

By applying tonal contrast to this fleur-de-lis design (see pages 72, 77 and 90) – below – and the Cornucopia (see pages 82–3 and 91) – opposite – an increased depth and quality has been simply achieved.

26

background shining through. (Begin with the darker area when painting, fading the paint out towards highlit areas.) Tone windows differently when they represent the two sides of a twisted form like a ribbon or leaf – lighter for the top, darker for the underside.

Combining colours

With very few exceptions, the stencils in this book avoid the laborious technique of superimposing two or more separate stencils each representing a different colour. This is partly because I dislike flat, ready-mixed colours, and prefer, instead, to allow my tones to blend in the actual stencilling process. Rather than stirring together a pink and a blue to make a consistent mauve, for example (or selecting a single mauve spray paint), I use both pink and blue in overlapping and merging areas, allowing the two to blend visually. It's a precedent set by the Impressionists, after all, and

the result has a translucent, dynamic quality.

Choose colours inspired by furnishings in the room. On something like a repeating swag border, I often work with a 'palette' of five or six colours in a harmonious range, using only three colours at a time for the stencil and changing one of them for the next repeat. Sometimes the tone modifies in response to a colour change in that part of the room: the pink in a flower garland stencilled around the walls might warm to apricot in the vicinity of a warm-toned sofa, perhaps.

In these single, multicoloured stencils, I often spread paint into an adjacent window. For example, the red of an apple might 'blight' the adjacent leaf slightly, just as some of the green of the leaf tinges the red apple. This happens in nature, and by doing the same when stencilling, you will find that your finished designs are simply and enormously enlivened.

27

COLOURED BACKGROUNDS

One factor that is very often overlooked is the effect a coloured ground will have on stencilled colour – particularly when this is as hazy and delicate as I like it to be. A pure blue painted on a yellow or even a greenish background takes on a distinctly green cast. (Blue also turns greenish under the influence of a yellowing varnish.) It is important to test your effects not only on a piece of scrap paper but on the ground colour, too, if this is anything but white. If you are planning to protect your stencil with a coat of seal or varnish, test this too, in case it alters the tone in a way that you don't like.

Obviously the background colour will greatly affect the colour you choose for your stencil. Always practise on some lining paper – and don't forget to paint a wash of the background colour first (if practicable) so that you can really see the finished effect.

SPRAYING

All crafts and do-it-yourself authors begin by advising you to do test samples first when experimenting with a new technique. Be warned: for spray paints in aerosol cans, this advice needs ten-fold emphasis. You can afford to do literally tens of samples on lining paper to get used to the feel of the spray can; to observe the different density of spray produced when the pressure on the nozzle is varied; to experiment with aiming the spray in different directions, and to get to know the way the spray can behaves. At the same time, you will also be discovering the most flattering way of colouring your particular stencil design.

Some experts describe the spraying process as disarmingly simple. I prefer to be realistic. The paint fumes make it rather an unpleasant business, and the aerosol cans themselves have a nasty habit of spattering, clogging or even running dry when you have just got into your stride. It is also not always easy to keep the lightness of touch you need in order to produce a gentle mist of hazy colour.

Don't be put off by these dire warnings, though. With practice, you will soon overcome any initial difficulties and there really is nothing like spraying for beautiful and subtle stencilled effects achieved at speed. I use it all the time and find that the versatility which sprays provide endlessly satisfying.

How to spray

1 Stick the stencil closely to the surface (repositionable spray adhesive avoids seepage), checking position by measuring.

2 Use tape to mask off any windows that you don't want coloured.

3 Protect the surrounding area with newspaper held in place by masking tape. On a vertical surface it is a good idea to fold the newspaper below the stencil into a sort of 'shelf' to catch downward-drifting paint.

4 Work by directing the spray towards a 'guard' and letting the paint drift on to the stencil. Hold the guard at right angles to the stencil and curve it to isolate the area of stencil you are working on.

An advantage of using sprays is that colour can be subtly built up. The stencils on the kitchen cupboards featured in Country Cupboards (see pages 43 46–9) are built up using three colours – red, rust and grey brown – as shown above.

Using sprays

There are many advantages with this medium:
- Rapid. Dries immediately: no waiting for paint to dry before repositioning stencil or changing colour; no seepage or smudging
- Capable of beautifully subtle fine haze of colour
- Versatile: compatible with most surfaces (apart from oil-based paints)
- Wide range of colours, including metallics
- Widely available in car accessory shops and garages

Hints
- A succession of fine coats enables you to build colour up gradually or to blend different tones effectively.
- Use a 'guard' – a piece of card the size of a foolscap envelope, or even an envelope itself – to localize the spray and direct it at a particular window.

- Work on darker areas first. For three-dimensional effects, grade colour from deep shaded areas (towards the base of a 'solid' shape, or on the side farthest from the light source), in order to 'highlight' areas where the ground colour shows through.

BEWARE

Spray paints can be toxic. Always read the manufacturers' instructions printed on the can before you begin. Above all:
- Work in a well-ventilated space, away from naked flames
- Avoid inhaling the fumes – wear a face mask
- Keep spray paints away from babies, children and pregnant women

---

Using brushes

The more traditional alternative to spraying is to apply colour using the special-purpose, blunt-ended brushes with stiff bristles described on page 19. What is not so traditional is the range of paints now available: their chemical constitution makes them quick-drying and so easier to use, and also suits them for particular surfaces such as fabric or tiles.

Colour specifically designed for brushing with, comes in varying forms, including stencil crayons and pots of liquid paint.

Brushing is particularly good for images with fine detail. Paint is applied very dry, with a dabbing, stippling motion that permits you to build up colour gradually and makes good clean lines around the image. The control you have with brushing permits you to achieve multicoloured images without a good deal of masking or the use of multiple stencils. Good control of colour grading is possible provided you avoid mixing colour and consistency.

Brushing is, of course, slower than spraying in achieving larger-scale results, though for people who find the pressures of the aerosol can too much of a challenge it can be quite soothing.

Choosing paint for brushing

Both acrylic paints and crayons are suitable for most surfaces – paper, paint, wood, plaster, etc. Check with the manufacturers' notes on the label if in doubt about the compatibility of a given material, and always carry out the necessary preparation of wood, etc, first.

Acrylic paints and crayons are not permanent on ceramic surfaces, however, and paint specifically sold for this purpose should be used for stencilling tiles.

Liquid paints

Acrylic paints are designed to be quick-drying. They are available in small pots from artists' suppliers, etc, as well as from specialists in stencilling equipment. There is a good range of colours, including metallics.

Using liquid paint is more like conventional painting, but it is essential to keep the brush almost dry, and to apply paint in thin layers, building up colours slowly with a cloudy, translucent quality.

Keep colours in separate blocks on your palette and blend them as you stencil. It *is* possible to use emulsion paint, but since it dries slowly there is a greater risk of smudging.

Stencil crayons

This convenient colouring medium consists of oil-based paint in stick form. Crayons are obtained from specialists in stencilling products. They are relatively expensive but come in a useful colour range and you can buy them singly. Above all, they are very easy to use.

Hints

● Make sure brush is clean and perfectly dry before charging with colour.
● Use a different brush for each strong colour contrast or for light and dark if you are *not* allowing colours to blend into one another.
● Practise samples on lining paper before embarking on the real thing.
● Keep brushes moist for *short* periods by wrapping bristles in cling film.
● Wash brushes or clean with appropriate solvent immediately after use.
● Keep bristles straight after washing and during storage with an elastic band.

LIQUID PAINTS

Using a brush – in this case for ceramic paint – is so accurate, there is no need to mask off adjacent windows when colouring only part of a stencil.

STENCIL CRAYONS

1 Break seal by rubbing on kitchen towel, then rub crayon on to a piece of stencil board: you could use a free corner of your stencil. Use this as your palette and work colour into your brush with a dabbing motion.

1 Ladle a little paint on to your palette (this can be a foil or polystyrene food dish) and take up a little colour into your brush. Make sure the bristles are almost dry and test first.

2 Work colour into appropriate areas of the stencil motif with a dabbing motion, making sure the brush gets well into the edges of the windows to make a clean line.

2 Work colour into the appropriate areas of the stencil motif with the same gentle dabbing motion. Build up the required depth of colour gradually.

3 It is always advisable to use a second stencil overlay for very detailed work. If applying a strongly contrasting colour, it is best to use a different brush.

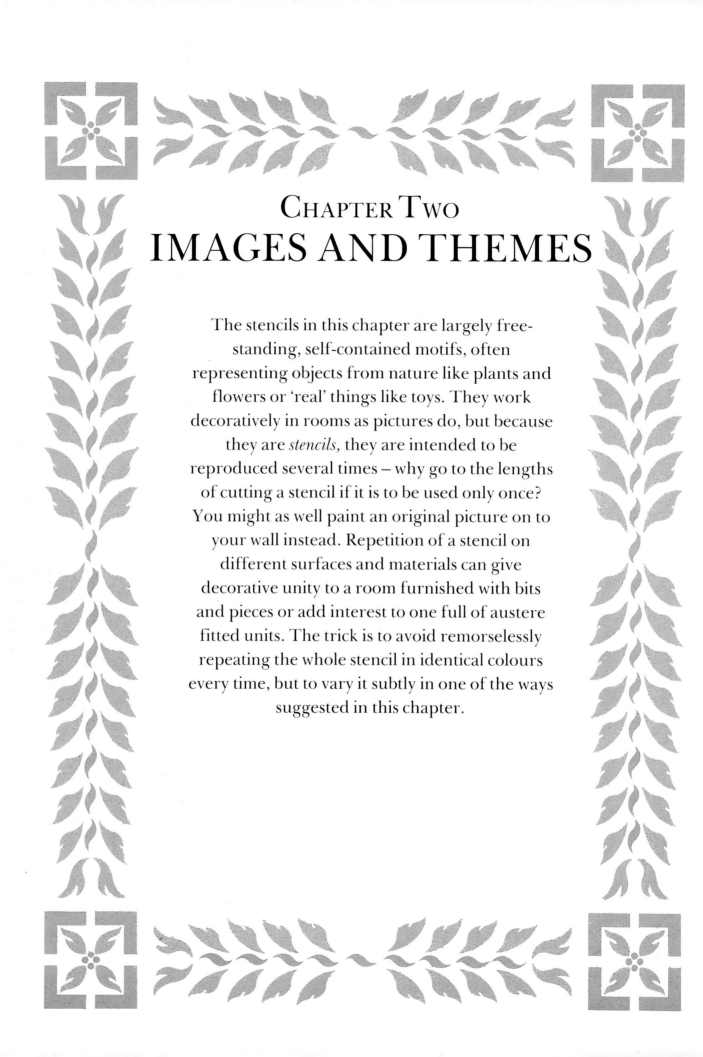

CHAPTER TWO
IMAGES AND THEMES

The stencils in this chapter are largely free-standing, self-contained motifs, often representing objects from nature like plants and flowers or 'real' things like toys. They work decoratively in rooms as pictures do, but because they are *stencils*, they are intended to be reproduced several times – why go to the lengths of cutting a stencil if it is to be used only once? You might as well paint an original picture on to your wall instead. Repetition of a stencil on different surfaces and materials can give decorative unity to a room furnished with bits and pieces or add interest to one full of austere fitted units. The trick is to avoid remorselessly repeating the whole stencil in identical colours every time, but to vary it subtly in one of the ways suggested in this chapter.

Just as you choose a focal point in a room to hang a striking picture, so stencilled decoration needs to be strategically positioned. Unlike pictures, which are removable, a stencilled motif becomes part of the shell of the room and should make sense architecturally. Relate the positioning of a purely decorative stencil to strong features in the room, centring it on a chimney breast, for example, or above a key piece of furniture. Link the subject matter and style of the stencil with the contents of the room so that it seems to belong and enhances what is already there rather than introducing some new and foreign element.

At the planning stage, try to 'read' your room for the best places as well as for suitable images. Realistic images have a potential *trompe-l'oeil* wit that you can often exploit by careful positioning. A hanging basket stencil or a bunch of herbs or dried flowers needs to be suspended from something: a beam combines the right sort of strategic support with the right sort of farmhouse ethos. An animal – be it a cat or a teddy – needs somewhere comfortable to sit. A potted plant, too, needs a sturdy support: stand it on the floor, the skirting board, a mantelpiece – not in mid-air. Other stencilled forms defy gravity, and you can decorate empty wall spaces as freely as you like with flying birds, butterflies and aeroplanes, with floating balloons and parachutists, or with moons and constellations of fixed stars.

I am a firm believer in positive stencilling. Don't use a stencilled motif apologetically or furtively, as disguise – to cover up ugly pipes, for instance – since it will only draw attention to that area. Tread boldly: by using stencils to create impact the eye will be attracted towards the decorative stencil and away from the ugly corners.

Use stencilling to marry together

Inspired by the activities of the teddy bear (see page 56), you can manipulate other figures. This marionette can sit, stand, dance or wave – all by adjusting the stencil's angle and by appropriate masking out.

disparate elements of a room. Because it is a stencil, be sure to use it more than once – and on furniture and fabric as well as on walls. Make the repeats slightly different each time. Colours can mutate to associate with different tones in different areas of the room. Motifs can be angled differently or reversed. Sometimes there are ways of varying the stencil itself, by masking off different windows and isolating parts of the design. Sometimes masking or adding-on will shrink or stretch the same basic stencil to fit panels of different-sized cupboard doors and unify a kitchen, for example.

Alternatively, use localized stencilling to designate different zones in multi-purpose rooms: the eating area in the kitchen might become a leafy patio or conservatory, distinguished from the work zone by stencilled potted plants and curtains of trailing leaves hanging down the walls, and perhaps spreading over the ceiling. Different stencils could create a restful mood in the sleeping corner of a child's playroom-bedroom and a more stimulating atmosphere in the play area.

It is often in children's rooms that people feel most licensed to stencil. The exuberant forms of toys plus the freedom to use bright colours without marring any tastefully toning décor offer plenty of encouragement. There is also the enthusiasm and appreciation of the incumbents: a sympathetic teddy sitting companionably on the wall beside a nappy-changing surface promotes comfort, and a frieze of animals just above the skirting board gives a crawling infant a welcome change from an endless succession of legs supporting humans or furniture.

Bear in mind the child's-eye view. In a baby's room, indulge yourself, too: all too soon the little angel asserts independence of mind with demands for Spiderman or David Bowie on the walls.

Both children's rooms and kitchens share the need to be practical – surfaces should be tough enough to withstand wear and washing. You might consider a coat of protective polyurethane varnish over the entire wall in areas of heavy traffic. In kitchens, though, be sensible. Although ceramic paints make it possible to stencil on tiles, avoid decorating near the cooker: hygiene and fire safety outweigh appearance.

Stencilled flowers hanging in bunches are reminiscent of herbs hung up to dry – but sustain the flower theme decorating the entire kitchen (see page 52).

PARACHUTES AND PLANES

Perhaps because they are airborne and naturally seen at this sort of angle, parachutes and planes make excellent free-standing wall stencils.

Stencilled decoration need not be pretty-pretty, but can draw on any kind of imagery that appeals, and can reflect all kinds of enthusiasms. In this older boy's room, parachutes and aeroplanes were designed based upon references supplied by the occupier himself. The parachute makes an ideal stencil, the whole ribbed structure and its cord forming a network of windows and bridges. By varying the angle of the image and the density of colour and reversing the stencil, a single stencil seems like more than one.

Planes offer images that translate well into stencils, with plated sections and rivets affording natural segments and windows.

FRIEZE FRAME
Featured on pages 78–90.
Instructions for using this
double stencil are on page 17.
The dotted lines indicate
where the next repeat should
be positioned.

FRIEZE FRAME
Featured on pages 78–90.
Instructions for using this
double stencil are on page 17.
The dotted lines indicate
where the next repeat should
be positioned.

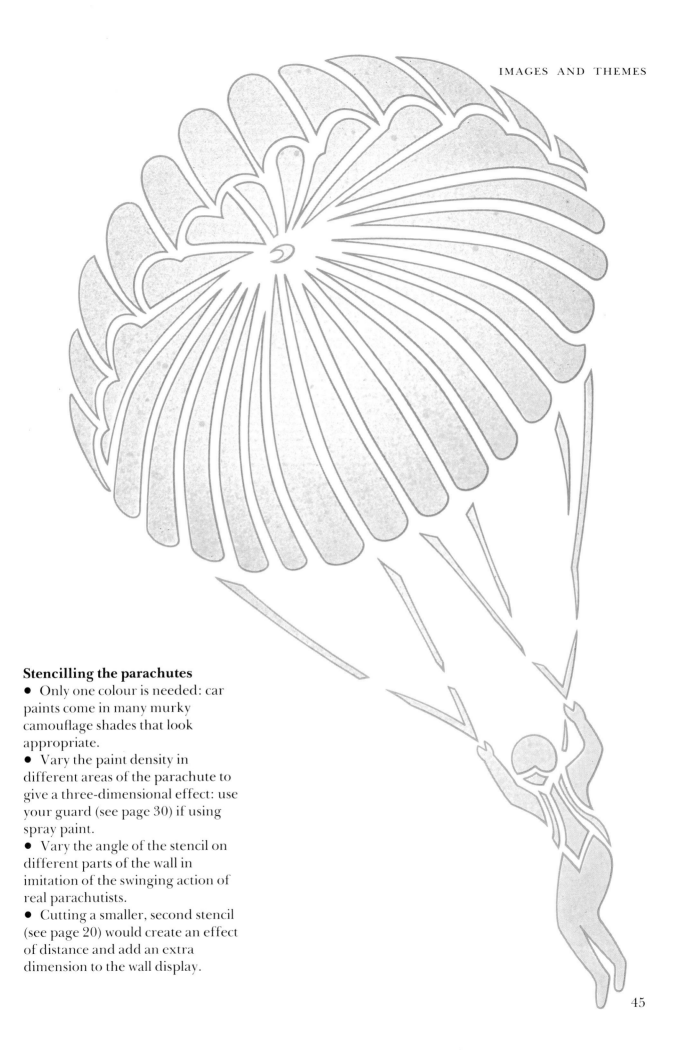

Stencilling the parachutes
- Only one colour is needed: car paints come in many murky camouflage shades that look appropriate.
- Vary the paint density in different areas of the parachute to give a three-dimensional effect: use your guard (see page 30) if using spray paint.
- Vary the angle of the stencil on different parts of the wall in imitation of the swinging action of real parachutists.
- Cutting a smaller, second stencil (see page 20) would create an effect of distance and add an extra dimension to the wall display.

COUNTRY CUPBOARDS

SEE STENCIL ON PAGE 43.
*On taller cupboard doors
the entire stencil is used*
(below) *On smaller ones*
(opposite) *the sprays at
the top are masked off, but
decorate the tiles.*

A stylized, Victorian inspired, leafy motif was chosen to enliven the bland surfaces of this kitchen and counterbalance the strong pattern of the tiled floor (see page 48). The angular shapes of the motif recall the chiselled effect of carved bas-relief and make an appropriate decoration for the grainy-textured bleached pine woodwork. The colours, chosen to warm the neutral tones, were built up from spray paints in red, rust and grey-brown and the natural variation that occurs with spraying prevents the repeats from being static in their repetition. The photograph on page 32 clearly illustrates how the colour was built up on these units.

As in the 'Fistful of Flowers' kitchen (see pages 52–55), the surfaces to be stencilled were of different sizes. I therefore designed this stencil so that the basic shape filled the smallest cupboard doors, and radiating sprays added height and width for larger areas. On the door of the tallest cupboard, two motifs were repeated end to end, and the sprays themselves made a scattering of less formalized pattern on incidental surfaces such as tablecloth and tiles. The flourish forming the base of the stencil was repeated to make a border for the Roman blind (see photograph overleaf). This wide range of effects is produced by using several of the many different elements of this single, versatile stencil.

It is often rewarding to doodle with parts of an elaborate stencil like this to see what a variety of patterns can be produced. By repeating shapes in a regular rhythm or in a random way, by interlocking alternate versions to make borders, and so on, you will soon discover many ways to alter the look of the original. All these different patterns will work harmoniously in a room because they are all derived from the same original stencil.

Repeating the main stencil establishes a rhythm throughout the kitchen, but variations prevent monotony. Elements of the design provide an emphatic border for the blind and a light scattering of motifs have been sprayed over tablecloth and tiles.

Planning to use the stencil

● Measure and draw scale outlines of all the different shapes which you wish to decorate. Sketch the different ways in which you will use and adapt the motif.

● Cut the stencil outline so that the main shape fits comfortably into the smaller of your cupboard panels. Stencil the little sprays at the top where space permits.

Colouring the stencil variations

● When spraying, mask off unwanted windows with tape to prevent colour from touching the surrounding surfaces.

● When brushing you have greater control over the paint, and you can usually apply paint locally – just through the windows you want to use.

● Use fabric paint (see page 116) for the tablecloth and blind.

● Use ceramic paint (see page 35) for the tiles.

PUSSYCAT, PUSSYCAT

Some stencil images seem to call for a support. A plant in a pot, for example, shouldn't defy gravity and float in mid-air – it ought to stand on the floor, or on a shelf – it can, of course, be a stencilled one. This pussycat is sleeping so comfortably it asks to be put somewhere nice. I know one little girl whose allergy to cats prevented her having a real one, but she derived great consolation from having this pussy stencilled alongside her bed. It is an easy option for anyone who doesn't approve of pets in bedrooms. And if it doesn't offer the benefit of purring, it won't wake up and scratch, either.

This is such a basic shape it calls for no subtlety of colouring – you don't have to cope with any shading

for three-dimensional effects, and neat primary colours straight out of the pot would not be amiss. The windows are small enough to make brushing with paint a realistic option – quite quick and painless to do. For simple variety, stencil a pair of companionable cats facing each other by reversing the stencil. A line of cats – facing the same way or alternating – would make a friendly frieze. Alernatively, stencils cut in different scales (see page 20) might make a cat and kittens.

Stencilling a pair of cats

● Mark centre position and stick stencil to one side of this, facing centre. Colour. Perhaps you could stencil the pair in different colours, or even just their whiskers, paws and the tip of their tail.

● Remove stencil, spray adhesive on second side and stick on wall facing the first cat. Check that the windows line up so that the bottoms are even and also that both pussies are equidistant from the centre line. Colour the second cat.

SEE STENCIL ON PAGE 75. *The same simple stencil reverses to make a pair of cats facing one another, but you could repeat the stencil in the same direction to form a queue, or you could stencil just one by itself.*

A FISTFUL OF FLOWERS

SEE STENCIL OVERLEAF.
Opposite: *The subtly distressed paintwork of a cupboard door frames the bunch of flowers like a botanical print.*

Above: *Stencils are reversed for symmetry on paired cupboard doors, but the colouring is not identical.*

The starting point in this newly modernized kitchen was a range of sober cupboard doors – a set of blank rectangles of different sizes and proportions, looking like so many picture frames waiting to be filled. The owner of the kitchen had said that she would like a breath of the country, something casual stencilled on to them – 'as if a child had just handed me a bunch of flowers.' Since freesias and roses were her favourite plants I based my design on them. In someone else's home they might be other kinds, or you might be prompted by some decorating element in the room: the china in this kitchen could inspire a wide range of ideas, though they would demand a more stylized treatment.

I sketched a simple bunch – just a few stems of freesias and roses, loosely knotted together – and planned the size of the stencil to fit just nicely within the frame provided by the smallest cupboard doors.

The way in which the flowers were stencilled makes an effect that is both casual and systematic. Where two doors make a pair below the sink and the cooker, and on either side of the oven hood, the stencil is reversed from left to right for symmetry. This symmetry is not carried through into the colouring, however. Although the leaves are consistently blue throughout, the flower colours explore a range from dull yellow to deep rusty brown. Because of the varying density and colour effects of the paint (and because the motif itself is so free) the paired stencils don't have a static and obviously symmetrical quality – in fact, the eye is constantly travelling back and forth, comparing them to make sure each uses the same repeated outline.

A further permutation occurs on the taller cupboards to the left of the window, where the bouquets are staggered, reversed, and hang upside down, like a bunch of drying herbs – another possible kitchen theme. A scattering of butterflies and dragonflies intrudes from another stencilled scene that is out of sight, but sustains the fresh-air, country atmosphere.

It is easy enough with an informal design like this to mask off a stem here or a flower-head there and alter the overall shape to fit the

design into a shallower or narrower space. Conversely, you can extend the design by masking off all but the odd spray and adding this to the completed stencil.

It is just this technique – of masking off and isolating one or two flower-heads – that has been used in the narrow space above the cooker.

Varying a repeating image
● Work with a 'palette' of three to five related colours and vary them subtly on different surfaces. Consider relating the colouring of (say) the flower-heads in a stencil to that of some other furnishing element in that part of the room.
● Mask off elements in some repeats for variety, or to fit the design into a differently proportioned space.
● When planning to reverse the stencil to make symmetrical pairs, it is usually easier to complete all the stencils facing in one direction first, then spray adhesive on the reverse side before completing all those running in the opposite direction.
● To make paired stencils balance, measure the position of each carefully from both the sides and top of the area.
● Do not feel that every last space has to have a stencilled image.

The overall effect is one of a theme that is
subtle and restrained – the flowers create a
distinctive atmosphere, but are not
slavishly repeated in the same way on
every surface.

BEAR FACTS

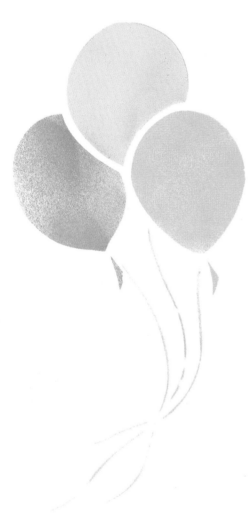

The dramatis personae of this tragedy are simple: teddies at child's-eye level and balloons in the air. You can simply use the sitting teddy on his own or repeat him in a line, with or without balloons. (You can also stencil balloons without teddies: a line of them in varying colour permutations makes a frieze which lowers the height of a tall room into proportions better suited to young children.)

Just slight variations can make a lot of difference to a teddy's frame of mind. The teddy's eye, nose and ear shading is on a second stencil that you superimpose on the main one, and you could change expression by altering this – or by drawing in a different face with a permanent felt tip. The sitting teddy can change position slightly if you mask off the head while you stencil the body, then position the head so that the teddy is looking up or down and stencil that, with the body masked off. You could adjust the angles of the arms and legs in the same way.

More dramatic changes of position make the upright teddy stand, walk or run, and wave his arms in the air: you just have to mask off different areas of the stencil each time. It is worth making a few sketches and perhaps practising on lining paper to plan the sequence before you begin on your wall. Work on the principle of starting with the arm and leg *nearest* to you, next stencilling the body and the head, then working on the farther arm and leg.

Stencilling balloons
● Concentrate colour towards the

SEE STENCIL OVERLEAF.
Every stencil here tells a story. The first teddy bear is sitting pretty with three balloons. The second teddy has only two, and is looking up in dismay at the balloon that is floating away. They third teddy is standing sadly with one balloon, and the fourth is furious – he has lost them all.

56

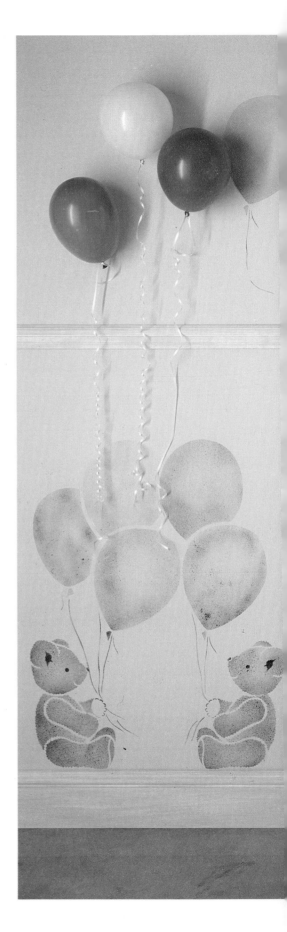

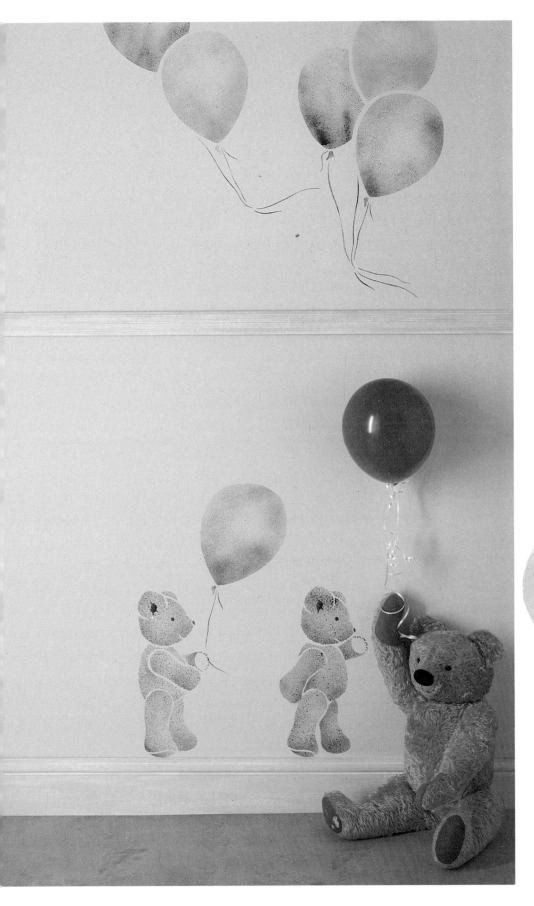

bottom and edges of the stencil window, keeping highlights at the centre to make the balloons look round and shiny.
● Mask off different balloons and their strings for variation.
● If the strings are being held by a teddy, mask them off behind the teddy's paw.

Stencilling the teddy
● Concentrate colour towards the bottom of each segment of the teddy to make him seem soft and three-dimensional.
● Colour the features in using the separate stencil in position over the face.

The teddy stencil outlines are in 'kit' form: if you want a lot of variations, cut separate windows for each shape and position and mask as you stencil. If you want to repeat identical teddies, cut your teddy ready-positioned in the right attitude.
Cut a separate stencil for the eye, nose and ear shading.

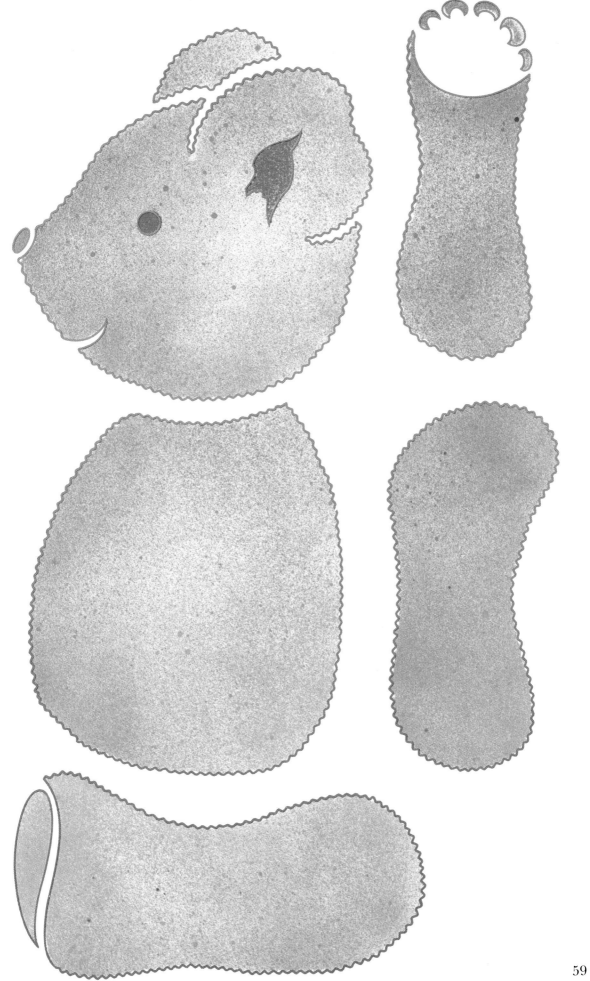

CHAPTER THREE
PATTERNS AND REPEATS

Repeating a stencil leads naturally to pattern. A line of motifs forms a border, a favourite decorative device. Repetition in two directions – horizontally and vertically – makes 'all-over' pattern. Pattern can be regular as clockwork or very free. It can consist of a succession of isolated motifs or a continuous interlocking flow. Traditional stencilling often uses pattern in a rigid, mechanical way, entailing a good deal of off-putting measuring and calculation. This is fine if you like that sort of thing: to my mind such strictly regular effects are best left to mass-produced and machine-printed wallpapers and border strips. A modicum of planning and measuring is inevitable with any repeating design, but only enough to achieve the visual balance that harmonizes with the setting. The repeating stencils in this chapter give a room individuality and life beyond the scope of any ready-made pattern.

The effects of pattern

Even more than with the pictorial images looked at in Chapter Two, stencils that are repeated as pattern seem to get absorbed into the surface they decorate and become part of it: stencil patterns on walls influence a room's whole architectural character. This is sometimes deliberately exploited, as when a stencilled architrave depicting a classical pattern has a *trompe-l'oeil* effect, taking on the three-dimensional quality of the moulded plaster it imitates. Architectural decoration is always more than just ornament: it is used skilfully to exaggerate and disguise. Think of the interior designer's portfolio of tricks – the way vertical stripes are used to give rooms an illusion of height (just as in clothes they are supposed to slim the wearer). The opposite effect is achieved by the succession of encircling horizontal lines –

skirtings, dados, picture rails and friezes – that break up the sheer vertical sweep of many lofty nineteenth-century interiors.

Modern buildings tend to lack this sort of inbuilt ornamentation, making rooms a blank canvas for decorating according to taste. Faking it with stencilled cornices and so on can compensate for that unfinished quality that bland modern interiors sometimes have, introducing a classical dignity or a softer-edged touch. Whether you are considering formal geometry or prefer something more natural is a matter of personal choice, though the existing character of the room you are considering needs to be fed into the equation too: a floppy, flowery garland would quarrel with a Greek key formality, but a more stylized leafy repeat might harmonize perfectly.

Handling a pattern repeat

In general, the more geometric and regular a repeating motif, the more scrupulous you need to be about fitting it into the available space. Some stencillers continue a repeat around a room willy-nilly, bending the obliging stencil board or acetate into corners as they come to them, or simply interrupting the pattern with white space as if cutting off a printed strip. I find a broken shape or an odd fragment at an edge or corner irritates like a snagged nail. It is far better to spend a little time adjusting a pattern to fit into the space exactly: you may need to re-space the repeats slightly or cut a special piece to make a 90-degree turn. A useful device is to fill a gap at the end of a repeat with a little motif or flourish borrowed from another part of the stencil or invented for the purpose. Quite often it is easily possible to adapt

A stencil around a favourite picture can highlight it while at the same time perhaps tying it into some other feature of the room. The stencil for this leafy corner is on page 94.

the stencil by masking it off as you work. Stencilling offers an infinite number of ways to turn a 'problem' into an inspired solution.

Balance and good visual pacing are equally important with informal repeats – especially swags, garlands, bows. Because these are large, strong shapes that 'read' clearly in a room, they can make you feel slightly queasy if their rhythm is not quite right. Here, planning is all the more important, both to avoid cutting off a repeat in its prime, and to make sure that the placing of the stencil works well with any major piece of furniture in the room. On the other hand, it is easier to adjust the spacing imperceptibly between repeats, making them closer on one wall than on another.

The usual plan – I'm talking about the plotting stage, *before* the actual painting begins – is to work outwards from the centre: see how many complete repeats fit into the expanse of wall, measure the remaining space and decide how best to make any empty space look like a graceful and considered pause rather than a gap waiting for something to fill it. Where there is some centrally placed focal point, like a chimney breast, a strong shape is best centred on this. The main thing is to 'read' your room so that your stencils work well in that shape, flatter its good points and detract from awkward ones.

If the space is interrupted by some major item like a door or window, particularly if this is set asymmetrically, think again about a continuous repeat. If making a pattern fit requires a great deal of juggling with measurements, it is easier to side-step the problem altogether. Perhaps the suggestion of an all-round border might be

better than the real thing. Occasionally when clients ask me to stencil a border around a room to help relieve a box-like plainness, I persuade them to accept a less constricting alternative. An angled stencil motif (like the one on the bathroom wall opposite) defines the corner and relieves the monotony – taking the eye outwards to the limits of the room – but without enclosing and defining the space too literally. Fragments, dextrously handled, are subtler; they are better in a small space because they leave the completion of the lines to the imagination. They can also work better in an irregular space or one with lots of eye-catching furnishing elements, which they can complement in a counter-rhythm of their own.

When you are at the planning stage of organizing a repeating pattern, it is vital to consider the room as a whole: you want to avoid the sort of scrambled effects described above that result from not being properly prepared. On the other hand, I have to confess that – after preliminary calculations to make sure everything will fit or balance in the general scheme of things – I sometimes modify my intentions when I'm doing the actual stencilling. Call it 'on mature reflection . . .' For this reason one of my unofficial tips is: begin with the most obvious parts of the room and then take a coffee break while you digest their impact. I have found that sometimes I decide that that is enough: continuing the stencilling round the corner or on to the adjacent wall is just not necessary. Or maybe I will balance what I have done with a slightly modified design somewhere else in the room. It is a question of understatement, and knowing when to stop.

ANGLES FOR IMPACT

These two trays – below and opposite – make use of corners in different ways.
Below: A strong corner motif has been incorporated and could just as easily be used separately.
Opposite: Alternatively, this motif has been adapted to incorporate corners.

One of the lightest 'architectural' stencilling devices takes the 'L'-shape, where two lines meet at a right angle, and uses it for subtle, but telling, emphasis. It is perfectly possible to put four corner angles together and make a closed square or rectangular frame. However, on the principle of understatement, the open-ended feeling generated by using one right-angle by itself is often just as satisfying.

The idea is architectural in the

sense that you don't use it in a vacuum but relate it to another right-angled shape. You can run a stencilled corner around an existing rectangle – a door, a picture frame, a mirror, a cupboard – where it quietly echoes and emphasizes that shape, perhaps softening its hard lines or relating it to other decorative elements in the room. Any frame is a device that contains an image and focuses attention on it; an extra stencilled

corner can form an additional framing motif – a gentle, asymmetrical gesture inviting you to 'Look!'. Depending on the situation, you could enclose more than one corner – two different angles overlapping one another, like the flowers and ribbons enclosing the little wall cupboard overleaf; or you could emphasize two opposite corners with a reversed motif.

As well as adding impact to an object that hangs on the wall, the 'L'-shaped stencil can play a purely architectural role on a wall or floor by delineating a corner or an area

Of course, you can easily use the Barley Twist stencil in straight lines only – it is simply one idea, oft repeated.

This pretty wall cupboard is attractively highlighted with the ribbons and flowers, reversed for symmetry. Note the tonal contrast to give the ribbon a three-dimensional effect.

of a room. A complete continuous border forms a boundary that fences you in and makes the space seem smaller, more confined; one or two corner markers seem to allude to the existence of a border but without putting a limit to it. In a box-like room with no ceiling mouldings, small stencillings pointing like arrowheads towards the room's corners carry the eye outwards, enlarging but nevertheless defining the room.

Emphasizing a corner
● Choose a design that incorporates a well-turned corner such as one of those featured here.
● Position the stencil so that both arms of the 'L'-shape are the same distance from and parallel to whatever you are surrounding.
● Relate the colour and pattern of the stencil to the room and the object it is supposed to enhance.

67

SWAGS AND BOWS

Conversions in older houses sometimes leave you with an odd wall that is a blank canvas for some kind of stencilling treatment. In this bedroom, one wall is a bank of panelled cupboards, and it was not possible to create a continuous effect around the room – such as a unifying stencilled cornice – to detract from the room's boxiness.

The main colour in the stencilled swags and bows links with both the sponged walls and the picture frames. A haze of blue-grey suggests a ribbon of rich moiré or shot-silk texture.

Instead, decoration is concentrated on one wall. A pair of eye-catching prints becomes a focal point at a height where the room's junior occupant appreciates them.

The 'dead' space above the pictures is filled with a series of dramatic bows (from which these two pictures seem to be suspended), linked by a swag of twisted ribbon. It is surprising how often scale can be challenged successfully: in a small space a single oversize stencil is often more effective than several small ones, and here the red tones make the motif an intrinsic part of the surroundings.

The idea and the scale may be dramatic, but the bows do nothing to lessen the impact of the graphic prints in their bold red frames: such a device would have to be used more cautiously – using paler colours – with less striking pictures.

The pictures must first be positioned as the starting point for planning a stencilling repeat of this sort. Obviously, the bows must be equally spaced and the swags evenly looped to establish a good rhythm.

Stencilling a series of swags and bows

● Bows are emphatic points and must be evenly spaced in relation both to a room's architecture and the pictures they 'suspend'. Measure your available space, mark the positions on the wall and see how well-balanced the bows/ pictures look overall. You may find it a good idea to adjust the proportions of the swag.

● Stencil the bows and swags alternately, reversing the bow from left to right on alternate ones.

● Use deeper colouring on insides of bows and on lower edges of swag twists to suggest three-dimensional shading.

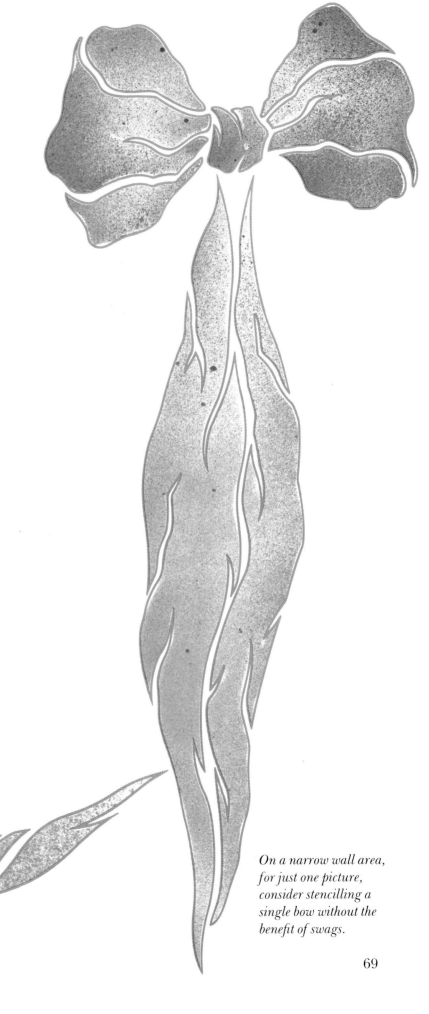

On a narrow wall area, for just one picture, consider stencilling a single bow without the benefit of swags.

69

ROSSINI FRIEZE

A room without intrinsic architectural features is given character by a stencilled frieze and dado effect.

The name for this stencil actually comes from the artist of the engraving hanging on the wall, but the design for the frieze originated in the moulding around the

fireplace in another part of this room. The stencilled repeat forms an abstract border pattern which has strong lines and vigorous movement reminiscent of waves

breaking on the sea-shore. It has something organic about it, too, suggesting a stylized plant form. However, all this primitive energy is confined in a narrow horizontal band, a disciplined effect, sufficiently civilizing the exuberance for a sophisticated town-house interior. You could further restrain it – and make a more grandiose border – by sandwiching the Rossini motif between simple geometric or linear borders such as the Barley Twist or Leafy Twist borders on pages 65 and 104. Its halfway character between organic exuberance and stylized discipline makes this border suitable for a wide range of building styles: it can either team with sober classical architraves and mouldings or stand alone, introducing dignity and distinction into otherwise characterless modern interiors.

The window wall in this room has a stencilled dado that looks like wrought iron railings, but actually represents a network of stencilled twists of ribbon. The inspiration came from some lace I saw hanging in a doorway in Brussels. The all-over stencilling was made from special stencils cut for the spikes from which the lace hangs, and for the curving twists at the bottom of the mesh.

The background has been rag-rolled in red on cream, creating a rich texturing behind the restrained black stencils. Distressed paint effects often make a wonderful surface on which to stencil, with a depth and movement of their own that particularly enhance the more abstract pattern repeats such as these.

Stencilling in Rossini frieze
● Measure each wall and plan the positioning of complete repeats so that no motifs are broken at the corners of the room. Adjust spacing if necessary, or devise a special 'filler' for corners.
● Enlarge the stencil outlines on this page to the required size.
● Cut the stencil parallel to the top of the stencil board or acetate so that this edge can be held against the ceiling to keep the border horizontal: this way it is unnecessary to mark the wall or to be constantly measuring.

While black is dramatic against textured paint on walls, this stencil can be given a much softer effect by using it as a double stencil with subtly differing shades to highlight the curves.

71

BLACK AND WHITE

SEE STENCIL ON PAGE 90.
A small city hallway (above) called for a simple but sophisticated stencilling treatment. Some iron railings by the front door suggested a fleur-de-lis motif, which was stencilled on one wall in a gradation of sizes (opposite). The smoky quality of the sprayed stencils softens the extreme contrast of black and white: motifs as solid as the floor tiles would be dazzling.

Since you plan a pattern in stencilling with a situation in mind, the result can have a particularly made-to-measure appropriateness. In this hallway, for instance, I decided upon eight different stencils of the fleur-de-lis theme cut to make the gradation from large to small up the wall. Don't be afraid to take time at the planning stage. Leave samples of your design – perhaps photocopied to different sizes – pinned up overnight or longer, and adjust their position occasionally, so that you keep getting fresh impressions of the effects of manipulating pattern differently in the space. The right way of balancing the pattern will soon strike you with that sense of appropriateness, and you can then plan the positioning of the stencils accordingly.

The fleur-de-lis motif has a timeless dignity that suits many houses, old and new, and different combinations of background and paint colour can evoke an historical atmosphere or seem fresh and modern. It is amenable to being used in directional patterns as well as freer designs.

Stencilling an all-over motif

The distribution of the stencils here was influenced by the presence of the picture as well as by the overall proportions of the wall surrounding the window. Take any such factors into account when measuring your wall for positioning.

● Mark a central vertical guideline on the wall. Mark horizontal lines for each row of motifs. Then, on each horizontal, mark stencil positions on either side of the central vertical, always measuring carefully. For a stencil like this fleur-de-lis which varies in size, I pencilled a small mark where the apex of the stencil window should go; if you were using the same motif throughout, however, you might mark the position for the corner of the stencil board.

● Attach the stencil to the wall in the first position, working from the bottom upwards. Mask the surrounding area and spray (see page 30). Continue for the remaining stencil motifs, making sure the stencil is vertical each time.

● Concentrating shading on the same segments of each stencil, as shown on the blue motif on the left, helps give the motif a three-dimensional quality and avoids a mechanical look.

72

**ROSSINI FRIEZE
AND LEAFY TWIST**
*Featured on pages 70-1
and pages 104 and 109.
Instructions for using these
double stencils are on
page 17.*

RIBBON
Featured on page 111.

BLACK and WHITE
Featured on pages 72 and 77.

BLACK and WHITE
Featured on pages 76 and 77.

RIBBON
Featured on page 111.

PUSSYCAT, PUSSYCAT
Featured on pages 50–1.

FRIEZE FRAME

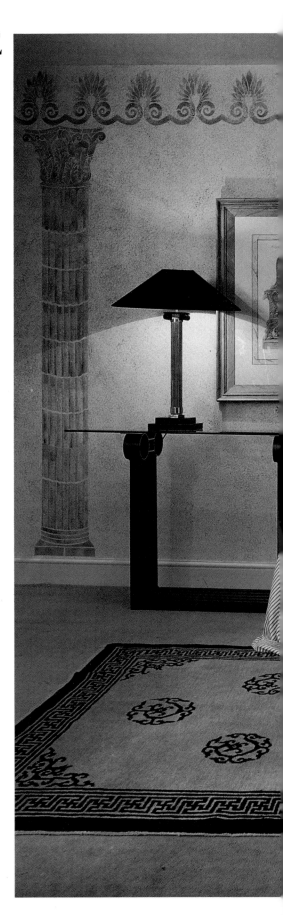

The inspiration for this border was an ancient Egyptian frieze. Contemporary interior designers can borrow from exotic cultures as shamelessly as archaeologists of the past raided the ruins of ancient civilizations, and the effect is, paradoxically, bang up-to-date. Mixing elements from different times and places is all part of the eclecticism of today's international style.

The sitting area of this potentially grand room is given a more intimate atmosphere where the frieze is 'supported' like a canopy by two Corinthian columns. Without being cosy, the framed space takes on a more human scale. (The low pool of light also helps to define and warm the area.)

The texture of stencilling here has a subtlety deriving from the fact that two separate stencils are superimposed on one another to build up the coloured shapes. The usual effects of sprayed paint – that hazy, uneven quality – are amplified with some shapes well defined and others mysteriously overlapping. The result is more shadowy and insubstantial than the usual one-layer stencil where a skeleton of bridges keeps the structure obvious.

Red and grey spray paints were chosen for the frieze, to go with the background – white paint liberally spattered with grey and blood-red. The colours blend and contribute to the soft, smoky quality of the plume shapes and the firmer rhythm of the scrolled base. An alternate colour scheme might exploit the flame-like effect of the motif and use reds and yellows.

SEE STENCIL ON PAGE 42.
Although this stencil is done in two stages, the two colours are not kept distinct but are allowed to blend. On the columns, particularly, this overlapping creates the effect of an ancient mural whose outlines have been blurred by time.

Stencilling the frieze

● Measure each wall and plan the positioning of repeats: at the end of a wall you can split this repeat centrally or between motifs without breaking the rhythm of the pattern.

● Trace and cut out the two separate stencils on page 42 (see page 17 for two-layer stencilling).

● Spray some practice motifs on lining paper to decide on the colour effects you want, and on which colour you will use with which stencil.

● Complete the positioning and spraying of the first stencil before you work along the frieze with the second stencil.

OAK LEAVES

Flourishing oak-leaves run along the wall in a dado effect, while more economical elements of the motif are stencilled in patterns elsewhere.

The strong horizontal line of a dado is a classic device for remedying proportion in a tall room. Here, the oak-twig motifs are at their leafiest along the dado (where they are backed by parallel lines), but sparser clusters and individual leaves and acorns stencilled on the wall and elsewhere sustain the theme. Classically, again, the motifs below the dado have greater visual weight than those on the wall above. In its organization this lower pattern is not random but systematically alternates reversed motifs in planned diagonals. The asymmetrical lines of the crossed twigs convey a sense of movement rather than of tight formality.

Adapting the dado-rail design

● First plan the spacing of your leaf stencils along a horizontal line – here the motifs are in pairs, with alternate ones reversed. Once you have established the spacing between them, cut a second stencil to represent the parallel lines of the dado rail, using the photographs here as a guide.

Above: *The dado strip works equally well as a vertical column, with the oak branches growing upwards in a leafy garland.*

CORNUCOPIA

SEE STENCIL ON PAGE 91.
Below: *Three repeats of the stencil stress the symmetry of the large dresser and lend it greater importance than a frieze would do.*

The cornucopia theme seemed natural for this large basement kitchen in a city house redolent of country nostalgia. Generous curving swags of fruit soften the slightly austere lines of the room. The spiral shapes echo a motif appearing around the fire grate, and are a classic ingredient in this sort of garland. Cool, faded-looking, purply blues tone subtly with the blue paint spattered on the pale green walls.

Instead of repeating the swag stencil in the obvious way, as a continuous border all around the room, we used it locally to give emphasis to strategic parts of the room. The vertical motifs above the fireplace are taken from a second stencil designed to decorate the full-length window shutters (not shown here), relieving the starkness when they are closed at dusk.

Stencilling the repeating swag

● Complete the central swag first (here, it was placed symmetrically over the dresser) and then position the others equidistantly on either side. Check that the measurement from the ceiling is constant on each repeat (measure to two parts of the stencil each time).

● If your frieze is to run continuously, measure the entire wall, and calculate the number of times the complete swag will fit into that length. If necessary, adjust spacing between repeats before stencilling to ensure that you don't end up with half a swag at the end.

Adapting the stencil for the chimney breast

● Centre the basic swag in the space.

● To widen the swag in proportion to the chimney breast, stencil part of the design that is an appropriate size and shape, masking off the main stencil. Here the spiral and leaf on the far right of the swag was repeated (at a different angle) at top right, and was then reversed and stencilled at a corresponding angle at top left. The stencil made for the shutters (not shown but based on this design) was also reversed to make two symmetrical vertical motifs at either side.

Opposite: *Over the fireplace the basic swag has been extended by repeating a leaf and spiral at either end. A separate stencil is reversed to make symmetrical drops.*

Chapter Four
FLOORS AND FURNITURE

Stencilling on wooden surfaces entails special preparation and finishing techniques, although the procedure for using stencils and applying colour is the same as usual. The natural graining and texture of wood adds a new dimension of depth to a stencilled design. On a floor this contributes a luxurious richness otherwise only available in far more costly materials. With a strong enough design, you can disregard the divisions made by floorboards or tiles: if the scale and proportions of the motifs are flattering to the floorspace overall, the design will transcend the materials on which it is painted. With furniture, on the other hand, designs have to be tailored or adjusted to suit the various facets of the piece. Cabinet-making is a precision craft, and just as drawers must slide smoothly and hinges hang square, so a stencilled border must fit immaculately and free-standing motifs must complement the proportions perfectly.

Floors

Stencil patterns for floors can draw on a wealth of inspiration from other traditional floor coverings. Some of the most attractive stencilled floors imitate the regular square or diamond grid of tiles in all-over patterns: the 'tiles' can be juxtaposed or separated and contained by borders – there are many permutations.

Children welcome floor stencils, from hopscotch grids and games boards to road-and-railway systems. Older ones might like the odd touch of *trompe-l'oeil* in stencilled footprints, tyre tracks and fallen leaves.

Planning From a design standpoint, the appearance of a room as a whole is generally more important than the details of the way the floor is laid. Take colour, proportion and design motifs into account in your floor stencils just as you would when choosing a carpet

The country motifs stencilled on to this chest of drawers have further enhanced its rustic appeal.

to complement existing features of a room. You can run an all-over design or a border across tiles or floorboards irrespective of where they join; or, if for instance your flooring already consists of well-laid tiles, you could base a pattern on these.

Preparing Since floor finishes must above all be hard-wearing, the best time to stencil is when a floor is new or has been newly stripped. The stencilled colour can then be applied easily and you can protect the floor with seal or varnish in one go. Old floors are often covered with a film of miscellaneous varnishes and polishes, and paint will simply not take on wax. In areas where it is impracticable to strip back to bare wood, remove any polish and try to adapt your design to the edges where it will not sustain much wear.

Stripping a floor is a fiendish task which involves hiring a large sanding machine that generates much noise and dirt: get someone to do the job for you.

Stencilling You can stencil directly on to stripped wood using spray paint, acrylics or wood stains, or you can first paint the floor and then stencil with paints. The sealing coat of varnish or polyurethane will darken or yellow both the colours and the wood, and can dissolve thickly applied spray paint, so try a test first. Wood varies in its absorbency, too, and trials are necessary to see how much paint or stain is needed to give the effect you want. Since stains are liquid, they can seep beneath the stencil and give a blurred effect.

Sealing Polyurethane seals, whether matt or gloss, are most highly recommended, although they may crack on a brand new floor which is subject to shrinkage and movement. Consider using non-slip yacht varnishes in bathroom and kitchen areas. Consult manufacturers' instructions for the number of coats to apply and the amount of drying time needed.

Wax, the traditional method of sealing, protects the stencil and the floor and looks good, but demands a prohibitive amount of upkeep.

Furniture

Storage units such as chests of drawers, boxes and cupboards, and even items such as tables and chairs, can be regarded as a series of variously-shaped and proportioned cubes whose surfaces invite decoration. A touch of stencilling will make both a piece of junk and a bland, functional purchase look at home by marrying them in with the colours and motifs in the rest of the room. Stencilling a unifying design on to miscellaneous pieces of furniture helps them work together. Stencilling on part of an item draws attention towards the pattern and away from less attractive areas, focusing, perhaps, on the top or edge of a table rather than on its clumsy legs.

Planning A number of regular rectangles within a frame, such as drawers or cupboard doors, may be stencilled with rhythmic repetitions of the same design. The repeats can be varied to give movement and interest as well as to cope with changing proportions. The gradation of drawer depths from shallow at the top to deep at the bottom offers an opportunity to 'build' with stencils, designing a narrow motif for the shallowest

drawer and adding on elements (such as extra leaves to a garland) so that the design works equally well on deeper drawers. Alternatively, the 'frames' themselves can be stencilled with narrow designs that exaggerate the outlines.

Designs can be free-flowing or geometrical, depending on your style. If you choose the latter, spend some time adapting the stencil to fit beautifully into the chosen space and perfecting any corner turns.

When your stencilled decoration is going to transform the character of a piece of furniture, pay attention to details such as locks, keyholes, hinges and handles. Fit new ones if necessary. You may need to remove fittings to stencil around them, adapt stencils to accommodate them, or even design special motifs to pick them out.

Preparing and finishing Where furniture is painted, spray paints and acrylics can be used in the usual way. It may be a good idea to protect any stencilled surfaces that are likely to be subject to heavy wear with a coat of appropriate seal – for example, chairs, table tops, cupboard doors.

If you want to stencil on unpainted wood, the principles are the same as those for floors. You need to make sure that you have removed any traces of wax, paint or varnish from the surface – a less daunting task than with a floor. It is fairly easy to get furniture stripped professionally by dipping it in a caustic bath; you can scrub wax off small areas using steel wool dampened with methylated spirits. Both the stencilling and the sealing considerations are similar. In addition, great satisfaction can be derived from polishing a piece of furniture by hand.

CARPET OF LEAVES

A small, fluid, all-over design is a practical solution for a bathroom floor. The size of the repeat makes it easy to stencil around awkward shapes, and continuing the pattern to the edges makes the space seem larger.

Three different leafy stencils have been used on this floor, but by reversing them and turning them this way and that, a greater impression of variety is gained. Although the stencil motifs are based on the grid pattern of the tiles, there are no hard edges and the asymmetrical design has a strong sense of movement. Bathrooms are often floored with cork – a rather dead surface – or with plywood 'mosaic' tiles in imitation of parquet, both of which invite stencilled decoration before they are finished with a protective coating of sealer or varnish. These tiles have enough interesting grain to add an extra dimension to the stencilled pattern, and the yellowing effect of the non-slip yacht varnish used in this bathroom contributes a warming richness of tone.

The leaf motif is endlessly versatile. Leaves can be stylized or naturalistic – you can copy motifs, design your own, or even use real leaves as the basis for your outlines.

Stencilling on wooden tiles

● Design your motifs to fit within the area of the tile. Three different motifs will prevent your needing to use identical ones side by side. Further variations result from turning and reversing the stencils.

● Make sure the floor surface is receptive to paint (see page 86).

● Attach the first stencil and mask off the surrounding area in the usual way, with masking tape and newspaper. Test the density of spray on spare newspaper before beginning to colour the stencil.

● Work from the far end of the room towards the door: although spray paint is quick-drying, this saves kneeling on work that has just been done. Work the complete motifs first; later, go back and work part-motifs on odd-shaped tiles around the edges. At the very end you may find it helps to cut a stencil to fit it around a particularly difficult pipe or corner.

● Spraying paint is rapid and easy, but remember to allow time after stencilling for the floor to be sealed for protection (check the manufacturers' instructions on the varnish-can for the drying time and the number of coats recommended).

SEE STENCILS ON PAGES 94-5.

The same basic shapes are used on the walls and floor, but whereas on the walls they are linked to flow in a loose linear pattern (opposite), *on the floor they are clustered into separate blocks to fit the tiles* (below).

*Stencilling tiles in a
bathroom or kitchen can
appear a daunting task.
However, a personal touch
can be achieved by use of
an occasional stencilled
tile, perhaps combined with
a complementary border,
(far left).*

95

IVY TRAIL

A mezzanine dining area links the kitchen and basement in this house. Part of it is used as a conservatory, and plants creep out into the adjoining rooms – real ones as well as their stencilled shadows – bringing the place alive as only plants can.

In a multipurpose room, blocks of stencils are useful for marking out areas of different use.

96

Ivy leaves make particularly fine stencil motifs. Their pronounced shape is easily recognizable, the veining adds to the design quality (while also providing strengthening bridges), and the lines of the twisting stalks contribute vigorous movement and direction. Just as real ivy is tenacious and goes – and grows – anywhere, so does its stencilled counterpart. You can mass several leafy stalks into a bunch. You can curve them into swags and garlands. You can repeat them into a border, reversing and altering the angle of the stencil, adding and masking out the odd leaf or berry cluster here or there. You can use odd, disembodied, leaves and sprigs, scattered at random or more systematically distributed over a surface in a regular pattern.

Nor do plant stencils have to be just plain green: look at the range of colours nature offers. Ivy, in particular, takes on curious metallic shades of blue-black, brown and purple – ideal colours for spraying, and good for brushing too.

These examples show that stencilling floors need not be an all-or-nothing affair, with lots of squares to measure and complicated sums to do. Stencils look good localized on floors; adorning an empty corner; 'zoning' an area for a different use; wandering round the edges of a room – or even scattered about like blown leaves. For small motifs like these, the brushing technique would not be too laborious – as it certainly would on an all-over floor pattern.

Stencilling on a painted floor
● It is essential to make sure the surface is clean and dry before stencilling.

● Use spray paints or acrylics as you prefer.
● To stencil scattered leaves, mask off unwanted areas and stick stencil in position: a stencil made of lighter-gauge acetate is easier to use in awkward places, such as the angles of stairs.
● Both floor and stencil will need subsequent protection with several coats of appropriate seal or varnish (see page 86).

A trail of leaves, blown into corners where no feet tread, makes decorative use of the narrow angles of this staircase.

The ivy trail motif is free-flowing, and so sections of it can be individually traced and stencilled according to requirements.

SCREENPLAY

While the main purpose of a screen is to conceal something you don't wish people to gaze upon, it can also be decorative, providing an alternative feast for curious eyes in the meantime. Also, since a screen has two sides, stencilling offers an opportunity to create two contrasting moods. The dark side of the screen shown here exploits the drama of wild creatures against a black background; the reverse (see overleaf) is all serenity and light. As well as the unifying

SEE STENCIL ON PAGES 106-7.

The dark side of the screen contrasts a formal bordering device defining the corners with the free shapes of birds, insects and the tree with its snake.

oriental style, butterflies on both sides provide a linking theme.

A screen like this is simplicity to make: it is simply four panels of blockboard which have been painted or sealed and hinged together. Here black paint reminiscent of lacquer was applied on one side; the natural wood grain was left on the other. Stencilling on the dark side was done by brushing with acrylic paints, on the light side by spraying. After stencilling, both surfaces were sealed with varnish.

In a bold and free composition, the designs on both sides ignore the folds which split the screen into panels. On the dark side, though, a border motif defines the corners of four panels, containing the space like an open-ended frame. To have run the border all the way round

The flowering tree in its exquisite pot (left) is a pièce de résistance *of free stencilling: you can just see how some of the clusters of blossoms are repeated. Oriental imagery offers a wealth of inspiration for the practised stenciller to decorate a screen in a unique way.*

would have been too obvious – far less subtle and suggestive. A sort of inscrutable oriental cousin of a Greek key pattern, this border can be extended to varying lengths, as seen here, and its intrinsic 45-degree angles are ideal for turning corners painlessly. A related border pattern (the stencil is to be found ready-to-use on pages 106–7) is shown on page 118.

This screen expresses my own fantasies, and I suggest you include animal and plant motifs according to taste. Illustrations of chinoiserie offer plenty of themes to adapt.

These treatments are, of course, applicable not only to screens; ideas can be adapted to panels, furniture, flush doors, walls, even fabric.

The butterflies originated in this picture in my home. First they flew out and colonized the adjacent wall; later some migrated to the screen.

Stencilling the butterflies

● Trace the insect shapes off this page, sizing up or down if you prefer, and then cut the stencils.
● Mask and colour body and wings separately. These motifs are small enough to be convenient to brush rather than spray.
● Treat the insects as separate motifs: by altering angles, reversing the stencil and changing colours these six shapes will seem much more varied and numerous.

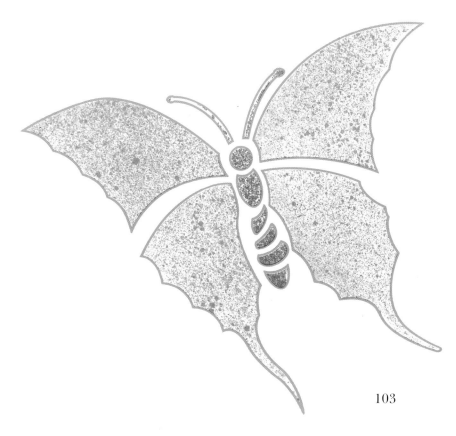

LEAFY TWIST

SEE STENCIL ON PAGE 74.
Opposite: A truly flexible stencil, here it has been used complete on the walls and details picked out on the sides of the trunk. The lid (below) shows how easily Leafy Twist can be adapted for corners.

A stone carving on an old church in France inspired this stencil. A stylized acanthus leaf twisting round a central column made a truly architectural support; even when translated into the flat image of a stencil, the motif has a strongly architectural feel. This is one of the most satisfying kinds of pattern, with the hard straight line of the shaft given softness and movement by the diagonal leaves, twisted so that they seem to wind around the column like a coil; it also makes a satisfyingly versatile stencil.

It is possible to repeat the entire motif end to end in a continuous horizontal line – perhaps as a border at cornice or dado level. Repeating it vertically in stripes makes a pronounced pattern (useful to give a low room an illusion of height). You get a nice fluid variation, too, if you reverse the stencil alternately, so that the 'twists' go in opposite directions.

The pattern makes a good four-sided frame or panel. It is easy to manage the corners by mitring the ends of the 'rod' so they meet at a 45-degree angle. You just have to plan the positioning of the leaves so that they are clear of the right-angles at the corners.

Finally, you don't have to use the stencil whole: both the leaves and the little pairs of berries make lovely motifs on their own. You could be systematic and space them out regularly, or scatter them at random over a surface. But they look particularly good held firmly within a bordering frame of the complete pattern.

Stencilling the chest top
- Make sure the surface is free from wax polish (see page 86).
- Plan the positioning of the border stencil and mark the corners where the borders intersect lightly with chalk. Then decide on the spacing of the leaves along each edge, and chalk their positions.
- Spray in the leaves using the first-stage stencil.
- Position the second stencil over the first, and use tape to mask off the corners at a 45-degree angle to make a mitre. Spray.
- Stencil odd incidents from the stencil in a random pattern over the trunk top and sides.

SQUARES AND RIBBONS

A simple grid of squares set on the diagonal floats on the black surface, suggesting a sophisticated pattern of pearly inlay.

Each piece of furniture presents a new challenge to the stenciller. There is the shape and character of the piece itself and the surfaces it offers for embellishment – with all-over patterning, odd trimmings, or border outlining. There is the background it will be set against, and the accessories that will complement it. Stencils need to conform to these considerations in both colouring and style – and, of course, they need to please the stenciller.

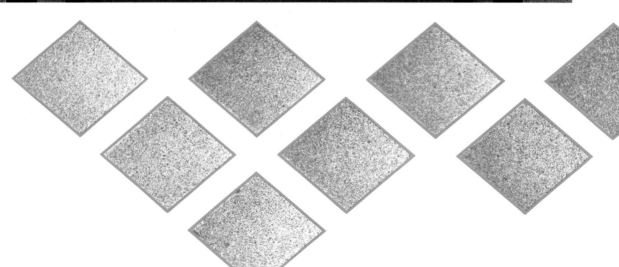

These two pieces demonstrate just how different stencilled results can be. On the black table, squares are stencilled like tiles, though their covering potential is hinted at rather than carried all over the top surface. The pattern of squares is also used as a border device. The result is asymmetrical, understated and subtle – the more so since the tonal contrast is not extreme. The accessories underline the sophisticated feel of the result.

A more exuberant and decorative approach turns the second-hand chest of drawers into an eye-catching piece. Deep blue was chosen to marry its rather stark whiteness into its setting, and the linear motif of a stylized ribbon border graphically outlines the main shapes.

Stencilling a pattern of squares

● Plan positioning so pattern is equidistant from edges. Since this is essentially a regular repeat, it is not possible to 'stretch' or 'shrink' it to fit odd spaces. Alternative options are either to cut different-sized squares, or to mask off the edges, thus ending with a row of triangles, rather than squares.
● Colour effects: repeat basic colour shading on each square (as here), or perhaps you could carry colour transition across a number of squares.

Stencilling a ribbon border

● Plan positioning so border is equidistant from edges. Adjust the number of 'loops' evenly along each side. Where repeats do not fit evenly, consider cutting a special central motif or corner piece.
● Create 'depth of field' by colouring the short 'ribbon' sections darker than the longer horizontal ones to imply a reverse side.

Extreme contrast of blue on white achieves a graphic effect as a stylized ribbon border outlines the different surfaces.

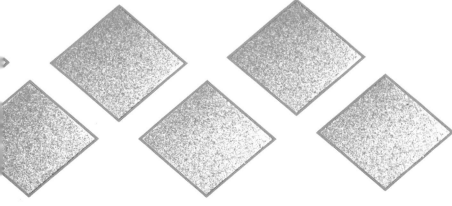

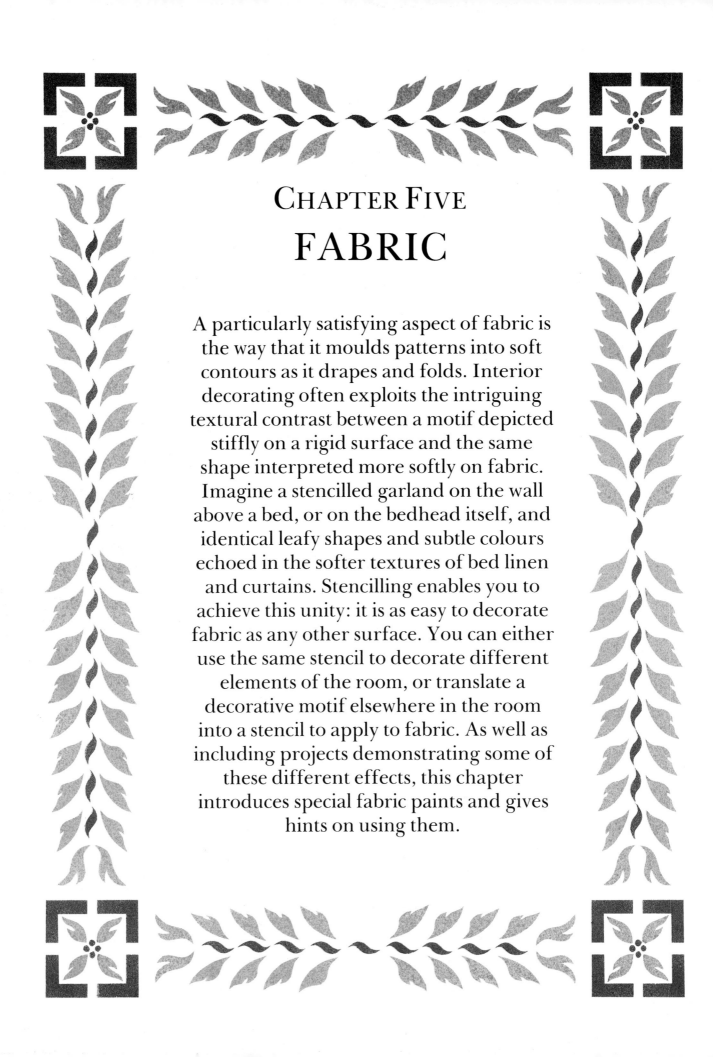

CHAPTER FIVE
FABRIC

A particularly satisfying aspect of fabric is the way that it moulds patterns into soft contours as it drapes and folds. Interior decorating often exploits the intriguing textural contrast between a motif depicted stiffly on a rigid surface and the same shape interpreted more softly on fabric. Imagine a stencilled garland on the wall above a bed, or on the bedhead itself, and identical leafy shapes and subtle colours echoed in the softer textures of bed linen and curtains. Stencilling enables you to achieve this unity: it is as easy to decorate fabric as any other surface. You can either use the same stencil to decorate different elements of the room, or translate a decorative motif elsewhere in the room into a stencil to apply to fabric. As well as including projects demonstrating some of these different effects, this chapter introduces special fabric paints and gives hints on using them.

Stencilled patterning has the same potential charm as printed fabric designs, with the added advantage that it is your own original work. The popularity of manufactured prints comes and goes in tides of fashion and it is easy to share the same date-stamped look with everyone else that season, or to dress your room in a fabric that advertises the identity of the designer or store as loudly as if the name were emblazoned across your curtains. When you stencil *you* choose the motifs, and position and colour them just as you please.

Be inspired by the way pattern is used in existing fabrics: as scattered motifs, all-over patterning, or borders that delineate shapes. Note where and how patterning is used successfully in different rooms. The key is to tailor your stencil patterning to enhance the finished object. Make fabric stencilling an exercise in composition: whereas when you buy patterned fabric the design is all-over and you often have to cut or sew through a motif to achieve the right fit, when

creating your own design you can make it work in just the way you want it to. Distribute motifs to follow the lines and curves of the fabric shape. Reverse stencils for symmetry of design. Position borders to complement the lines of the fabric. Adjust spacing to suit proportions. Stencil an all-over motif more densely towards the lower edge of an item, creating visual 'weight' at the bottom of, say, a curtain.

You can stencil on ready-made-up articles (provided they can be laid flat on a surface for stencilling: you'd need, for example, to open out a gathered or pleated frill). Or you can stencil the cut-out pattern pieces of fabric and sew them together later.

There are so many ways in which fabric contributes to atmosphere. Different textures behave in different ways, each suiting individual interior styles – translucent effects at curtained windows, for example, can be achieved in soft muslins or in diaphanous organdies, depending on whether the overall 'feel' of the furnishings is country/farmhouse on the one hand or more 'international' and sophisticated on the other; more substantial fabrics form solid sculptural curves (thick silks), soft pleats (medium-weight cottons), or crisp folds (smooth linen and fine, starchy cotton).

There are many exciting ways to use stencils on fabrics to bring added interest to a room. The butterflies (left) – see stencil on pages 102-3 – have been applied to canvas and then worked in needlepoint to make attractive cushions and the fleur-de-lis motif (right) adds the final touch to the hallway featured on pages 72 and 77.

The cornucopia stencilled onto these glazed cotton napkins uses colours reflecting both the autumnal and marine inspiration.

Preparation Consulting manufacturers' instructions, carefully launder fabric to remove any chemical finish that might make the fabric resistant to colour absorption, and iron smooth. If the stencilled design consists of a regularly repeated pattern, measure and mark the position for the stencil using pins or masking tape. It is important to be as accurate as possible. Sometimes pressing a light crease into the fabric is a good way of aligning a straight border.

Finishing Special-purpose fabric paints have detailed manufacturers' instructions on the label, but a reliable general method for fixing colour so that it is washable is heat-sealing. Allow the paint to dry thoroughly and then iron (without using steam) at a temperature appropriate to the fabric, running the iron for a minute or so over either side of the fabric. Alternatively, and providing the fabric will take the heat, place it in a tumble-dryer set at the hottest temperature for a maximum of 45 minutes.

Method

1 Lay the fabric to be stencilled out on a flat surface on top of a sheet of plastic, perhaps holding it in place with masking tape or clothes pegs.

2 Attach the stencil to the fabric using repositionable spray adhesive pressing it down evenly to give close contact all over the fabric surface and prevent the stencil from shifting.

3 Mix the required colours and decant some fabric paint on to a palette. Take up a little paint into the bristles of the stencil brush and then work the excess out on to a paper towel. Test the paint texture on a scrap of fabric before starting to stencil. For a fine fabric, you will need to add some water so that the paint absorbs more easily. The exception is silk: if the consistency is too watery, the paint will bleed beneath the stencil.

4 Apply paint to the fabric, working areas of 'shading' around the edges of the stencil windows first and building up the density of colour in the usual way. Use a firm jabbing action of the brush to work paint well into the weave so that it penetrates deep into the fibres.

CHINESE WHISPERS

SEE STENCIL ON PAGES
106-7.

Opposite: *Bamboo is an
ideal stencil subject. Its
jointed stems make natural
bridges, and the slanting
leaves give vigorous
movement to the design.
Both sections of stem and
leaf-clusters can be built
up to make longer and
more complex patterns.*
Below: *Square cushions
look good with all-over
patterning but are also
perfect shapes for outlining
with borders. The Chinese
key featured on the screen
on page 101 has been
adapted for use in just this
way here.*

All of these designs are oriental in
inspiration, but the individual
effects range from the disarming
casualness of the naturalistic
bamboo through the highly
wrought simplicity of the key
border to the serpentine intricacies
of the dragon design. The
whispered message is that there is a
stencil for every occasion: choice of
colours and textures plus the
character of the motif enable you to
marry your stencilled cushions to
any surroundings – simple or
opulent. Different designs work
together when they have something
in common: their oriental
derivation, or their repetition of the
same fabric and shape.

The square of a cushion cover
can be a canvas on which you stencil
an open-ended design, or you can
choose to emphasize the square and
its geometry with a precision-fitted
border. You can, of course, apply
these stencils in other contexts. A
cousin of this border decorates the
screen on page 101, and bamboo
transplants to any surface.

Stencilling on silk cushions
• Sandwich a sheet of plastic
between the two layers of the
cushion cover to prevent any colour
from seeping through to the
underside.
• Keep fabric paint (see page 116)
dryish in texture: silk is very
absorbent and diluted paint bleeds
readily behind the stencil.
• Avoid dropping water on the silk
– marks will be permanent.

Adapting the key border
It is easiest to use the wedge-shaped
'modules' of this design as they are
(see ready-to-use stencil on pages
106–7), and to choose a square or
rectangle into which they will fit
exactly. The essence of this pattern
is its regular rhythm, and it loses its
tightness if the separate units are
simply spaced more widely (as you
can do with free shapes).
• You can use the complete shapes
as building blocks to fit into spaces
of different lengths.
• You can shorten or elongate
sections of the blocks, keeping
proportions and style as close to the
original as possible.
• If you are contemplating any
such adaptation, do your planning
thoroughly (use photocopies and
tracings if necessary) before you go
to the length of cutting actual
stencils.

The basic stencil for this Chinese Key is on pages 106-7. The diagrams (above) illustrate just two of the many ways in which the elements of the key may be put together. Try experimenting yourself and see what happens.

BLUE
ROSEBUDS

The theme of rosebuds in this bedroom demonstrates the versatility of a simple plant form when used as a stencil. Here the basic motif, consisting of a sprig of buds and leaves, could simply have been stencilled whole, but since it is a long, directional shape, it has been repeated lengthwise for a narrow border on the small frilled cushion. Several repeats of the motif have been built up to make a spray, too, by masking off some leaves or buds and repeating others for variation. Also, parts of the stencil have been masked off so that different elements – isolated leaves or buds – could be scattered in different configurations.

Coloured in the same basic blue fabric paint (mixed with tones of violet or jade), the stencilled motifs unify a host of different items of soft furnishing and bed-linen. All of the stencilled items here were actually home-made, but, with the exception of the stencilling on the frill (which needs to be done before the fabric is gathered), everything could be bought ready-made and decorated at home. Tackle each item slightly differently: it is intriguing to see how many variations are possible.

Stencilling details on fabric
● Where stencil windows are sufficiently far apart, you may – with care – manage to colour details (such as the buds at the end of this stencil) without extensive masking. Both good-quality cotton sheeting and organdie, used here, are easy to stencil with fabric paint and a brush (see page 116).

Different fragments of the rose spray are stencilled on various surfaces: buds on the organdie drape cloth, leaves on the circular undercloth and on the sheers at the window. Note the tie-back decorated with the complete motif.

The circular tablecloth
● Since the drape cloth covers motifs on the table top, stencilling can be restricted to the skirt of the cloth.
● Insert a line of tacking or sewing pins in order to designate the limits of the area which is to be stencilled.
● Using full-width sheeting cotton prevents the need for any seams.

The small frilled cushion
● Stencil after joining the lengths of fabric for the frill, but before gathering them so that they can still be laid flat.

The sheer curtain
● The distribution of the stencilling is much denser towards the base of the curtain. The leaves fade out almost to nothing at the top, where most light comes through.

The tie-back
● Stencil the complete rosebud motif on fabric long enough to fold into a tie-back. Cut a piece of plain fabric to the same size, tack together the stencilled fabric and the lining, stitch around the entire shape (right sides facing), then turn right way out and pad lightly. Reverse for symmetrical tie-backs.

ACKNOWLEDGMENTS

The publishers thank the following for their help with this book:

Locations: The Chelsea Gardener (pages 13, 85, 100-2); Anita Eyers – Interior Designer (pages 10, 11, 52-5, 62, 66, 72, 77, 88, 93, 115); Tina Griffiths (pages 8, 39, 40, 83); Magnet PLC (pages 25, 31-3, 46-9).

Accessories: Alfrank Furniture Design: Benardout and Benardout; Conran Shop; Cork Street Framing; Designers Guild; Heal's; special thanks to the London Sofa Bed Centre, Tottenham Court Road; and Percy Bass Ltd.

LIST OF MANUFACTURERS

The following addresses are but a few of the many suppliers of the products included in this book. Your local arts supplies store, craft store or hobby shop will be able to supply the products and implements referred to in the directions and advise you on alternatives.

DMC Corporation, 107 Trumbell Street, Elizabeth, New Jersey 07206 and
Dunlicraft, Pullman Road, Wigston, Leicestershire, LE8 2DY
206 perle cottons, 430 4-ply wool colours, 100 2-ply colours, all the canvas sizes.

Dylon International, Stahlwood Toy Manufacturing Co, 58-80 Grand Avenue, Maspeth, Queens, NY 11378 and
Dylon, Worsley Bridge Road, Lower Sydenham, London SE26 3HD
12 fabric paints, 8 fabric felt tips.

Euro Studio, Unit 4, Southdown Industrial Estate, Southdown Road, Harpenden, Herts AL5 1PW
24 stencil crayons.

L G Harris, Stoke Prior, Bromsgrove, Worcestershire
Stencil brushes and touching in brushes.

Maestro Craft Colours, Unit 8, Whitebridge Lane Industrial Estate, Whitebridge Lane, Stone, Staffordshire ST15 8LQ
44 hard surface paints, in very convenient containers.

G Rushbrookes Ltd, Regal Way, Park Road, Farringdon, Oxon SN7 7BX
Gardening aprons, with useful clips when up a ladder.

G H Smith and Partners, Berechurch Road, Colchester CO2 7QH
18 hard surface paints, 42 ceramic paints, 15 fabric paints.

3M PLC, 3M Centre, St Paul, Minnesota 55144-1000 and
3M United Kingdom, 3M House, Bracknell, Berks RG12 1SU
Spray mount repositioning glue a must.

Carolyn Warrender, 91 Lower Sloane Street, London SW3
43 hard surface paints, 18 fabric paints, 10 ceramic paints
and all the brushes, cutting mats and equipment.

INDEX

Page numbers in *italic*
refer to the illustrations